SEEDS OF CHANGE

The Story of Cultural Exchange after 1492

Sharryl Davis Hawke

James E. Davis

A joint project of the
National Museum of Natural History,
Smithsonian Institution,
and the
National Council for the Social Studies

 ADDISON-WESLEY PUBLISHING COMPANY
Menlo Park, California • Reading, Massachusetts • New York
Don Mills, Ontario • Wokingham, England • Amsterdam • Bonn
Sydney • Singapore • Tokyo • Madrid • San Juan • Paris
Seoul, Korea • Milan • Mexico City • Taipei, Taiwan

This publication has been made possible through the generous support of The National Potato Board.

The "Seeds of Change" research, exhibitions, publications, and programs have been made possible through the support of the Xerox Corporation. Development of *Seeds of Change* educational materials has been a cooperative venture of the National Museum of Natural History, Smithsonian Institution; Science Weekly, Inc.; and the National Council for the Social Studies.

This book is published by the Addison-Wesley Innovative Division.

Managing Editor: Michael Kane
Project Editor: Mali Apple
Design Director: John F. Kelly
Design: Square Moon Productions
Original Artwork and Cover Art: Rachel Gage
Cartography: Krist Mathisen
Composition: Julie Bellitt
Production: Erin Livers, Arts & Letters
Photographic Research/Editorial: Leslie Burger

ISBN 0-201-29419-2

2 3 4 5 6 7 8 9 10 - **WC** - 96 95 94 93 92

Contents

To the Student

Dear Student:

Try to imagine a world without pizza, chocolate candy, and french fries! Even more difficult, imagine American farms without horses, cows, sheep, or chickens! Such a world existed and not so very long ago—500 years to be exact.

America as we know it today dates back only to 1492. In that year, the courageous navigator Christopher Columbus sailed west from Spain with three little ships, the *Niña, Pinta,* and *Santa María,* in search of the Indies. He found instead two great continents unknown to the peoples of Europe—North and South America.

By linking Europe and the Americas, Columbus began what scholars call the "The Columbian Exchange." This little-known story refers to the exchange of peoples, animals, plants, and diseases between Europe, Africa, and the Americas that began with Columbus. For example, Columbus and those who followed him brought, among other things, sugarcane, horses, and diseases to America. The sugarcane and horses were introduced on purpose. The diseases were introduced by accident.

Whether purposeful or accidental, the new introductions had an enormous impact on the Americas. Diseases such as smallpox, measles, and the common cold killed thousands of Indians who had no immunity to them. Horses, on the other hand, at first frightened the Indians, who called them "Sky Dogs." In time, Indians became some of the finest horsemen the world has known.

Sugar, introduced by Columbus on his second voyage, depended upon slavery to make it profitable. Although American Indians were readily enslaved, so many had died from disease that the Europeans turned to Africa for the people needed to work on the sugar plantations. The exact number of Africans kidnapped and sold in the Americas will never be known. However, estimates range from ten to twenty million. Africans not only made sugar production profitable, but they eventually replaced Indians as the largest ethnic group in the Caribbean and in parts of North and South America.

From the Americas, Europe, Asia, and Africa received a variety of plants, including the tomato, maize (corn), the potato, tobacco, and quinine. These affected the health and diet of peoples in every corner on the globe. Indeed, plants of the Americas like maize and potatoes are now nearly as popular as wheat and rice in Asia. People everywhere benefit from a variety of drugs derived from American plants that can cure many diseases.

The book you are about to read, based on the exhibit "Seeds of Change" at the National Museum of Natural History in Washington, D.C., tells this story. It represents the life's work of scholars from around the world. "Seeds of Change" is their interpretation of the true meaning of Columbus. It has been 500 years since that fateful day when Columbus, the Admiral of the Ocean Sea, stepped ashore in the Bahamas and unknowingly changed the course of world history.

Herman J. Viola, Director
Seeds of Change
National Museum of Natural History
Smithsonian Institution

1

A CHANCE MEETING
That Changed the World

In perfect rhythm, the Arawak fishermen rowed their dugout canoes to shore in the afternoon sun. Today's catch had been successful. On board were enough fish for several meals.

As they approached shore, the men saw that the village women had prepared a large fire on which to cook the fish. With their fish, the villagers would also have corn or perhaps sweet potatoes and fresh bread made from the potato-like roots of cassava plants. Roasted lizard would be a special treat. By the meal's end, the villagers had eaten all their stomachs could hold.

After eating, someone suggested playing a game. Off to the village playing field hurried men, women, and children. Players divided into two teams. One player started the villagers' favorite game by tossing a rubber ball in the air. The toss set off a hard-fought game in which players twisted and turned to keep the ball in the air—without using their hands or feet.

Opposite page: A Bahama island, like the island once home to Arawak villagers.

DIGGING UP THE PAST

The Arawaks who lived 500 years ago had no written language. Yet we know that they were excellent farmers and made fine pottery. We also know they enjoyed games. How do we know this without a written history?

We know about the Arawaks' life because scientists called *anthropologists* have studied objects left by these earlier people. Digging in the soil, anthropologists found pieces of pots, tools, and jewelry made and used by the Arawaks. They also uncovered sections of playing fields. Like putting together a giant jigsaw puzzle, anthropologists used these pieces of information to imagine life in early Arawak communities.

Above are drawings of Arawak pottery pieces. Choose one piece and imagine the dish or pot of which it was once a part. On your own paper, draw the dish or pot that you imagine.

As the sun sank behind the horizon, the villagers returned to their homes. Soon they were sleeping in their wooden huts. A gentle breeze blowing through the huts' palm-thatched roofs was the island's only sound.

For members of this Arawak village, the night was like many others in their tropical island home. As they slept, how could the Arawaks have imagined what drama awaited them the next day?

In Search of the Indies

Standing on the deck of his ship, the *Santa María*, Captain Christopher Columbus could feel the roll of ocean waves. Although it was after ten o'clock at night, the captain could not sleep. It had been more than two months since he and the men on this and his fleet's other two ships, the *Pinta* and *Niña*, had left their homes in Europe. They had seen no land in several weeks.

PACKING FOR THE TRIP

Columbus's crew left Spain expecting to reach the Indies. Everything needed for the journey had to be packed into the fleet's three small ships. The *Niña*, Columbus's favorite, was only about 70 feet long and 21 feet wide.

Pretend you had to decide what to take on the journey. List the things you would load onto the ship. Don't forget the crew! Compare your choice of supplies with the things Columbus took, as listed to the right.

cannon, salted meat, biscuits, sardines and anchovies, water, wine, oil, flour, garlic, onions, cheeses, dried peas, guns and gunpowder, ropes, 24 crewmen

Columbus had prepared almost ten years for this journey to discover a new route from Europe to the Indies. *Indies* was the term Columbus and other explorers used to include the present-day countries of China, Japan, Indonesia, and India. The captain's plan called for his European crew to sail west from Spain (in Europe) across the Atlantic Ocean. Once in the Indies, he believed he would find the spices, silk, gems, gold, and other precious metals earlier explorers had brought home to Europe.

The ship's crew did not share their captain's confidence. Two days earlier the sailors' patience had seemed at an end. Columbus had bargained with them to continue the trip. As he stared across the waves, the captain thought about the bitter defeat of failing to reach the Indies. How could he tell Queen Isabella and King Ferdinand of Spain that he was not able to discover a new route to the Indies after they had given him money to make the trip?

COLUMBUS'S LOG

Do you keep a diary or a journal? Many people have a special book in which they write important things about their lives.

Columbus kept a diary, or log, of his 1492 voyage. Nearly every day he wrote an entry, a few sentences about that day's travels. He described the ship's location, what he saw, and sometimes his feelings. Although many explorers before Columbus had traveled to faraway places, few kept travel records.

Columbus's 1492 log was lost, but we can identify his handwriting from many letters like this.

Columbus's handwritten log was lost after he returned to Spain. However, his son, Ferdinand, and a friend, Bartolomé de Las Casas, each rewrote the log. Their logs probably do not retell Columbus's story exactly, but they do provide us with some important information about the trip.

Think how Columbus must have felt when he finally saw land. On your own paper, write the entry Columbus might have put in his log that night.

Peering into the darkness, Columbus's attention was drawn to a tiny flickering light. As he continued to scan the horizon, the light appeared brighter. Columbus was sure the light could mean only one thing—land.

At about two o'clock in the morning, the lookout sailor aboard the *Pinta* began to shout, "Land! Land!" The *Pinta's* captain fired his ship's guns to tell the sailors that land had been spotted. The captain's hunch had been right! To avoid damaging the ships by running aground, Columbus ordered his sailors to lower the sails. In the daylight, they would sail toward the land.

Probably no one aboard the ships slept the rest of the night. With the rising of the sun, the three ships set sail toward the land Columbus believed would bring them wealth and praise.

The Arawaks and the Europeans Meet

In the morning light, the men stared intently at the land they had waited so long to see. Sailing along the coastline, Columbus realized that the land was not a large land mass but instead a small island. However, he was not discouraged. Having read the writings of earlier explorers, Columbus believed there were many islands offshore from the Indies. This, he reasoned, was one of those islands.

Finding a place to anchor their ships, Columbus and several of his top-ranking crew went ashore in small rowboats. The date was October 12, 1492. Columbus's first act was to kneel and give thanks to his Christian God for allowing the ships to reach land. He then named the island *San Salvador*, which means "Holy Savior." All this was written down to give the King and Queen on the return to Spain.

As Columbus and his crew claimed the land for Spain, they were met by the Arawak villagers on whose island they had landed. The Arawaks' name for their island was *Guanahaní*. In the hundreds of years they had lived on the island, they had built homes, fields, and recreation areas.

We can only guess what the Arawaks must have thought about the Europeans. They had never seen such

No portrait of Columbus was painted while he was alive. This painting shows Columbus as an older man, the time of life when he made his voyages.

This painting, entitled Columbus Landing at San Salvador, *shows its European artist's impression of the event.*

large ships rising out of the sea. Nor had they ever seen fair-skinned men, full-body clothing, guns, or writing paper and quill pens.

From Columbus's log, we know about his impressions of the Arawaks. We also know he named the people he met "Indians" because he thought he had reached the Indies.

Columbus wrote that he was struck by the gentleness and kindness of these people. Although they knew nothing about the strangers to their land, the Arawaks made no move to challenge or harm the visitors. Their appearance Columbus deemed "very well made, of very handsome bodies and very good faces." He described their hair as black and coarse, "like the hair of a horse's tail," and wrote that some painted their bodies in black, white, or red. He noted that they wore no clothing.

From what we know about the first meeting of Columbus's crew and the Arawaks, the encounter seems to

What Do You Think?
Why do you think Columbus believed he had a right to take possession of the Arawaks' island for Spain? Why do you think he renamed the island *San Salvador* rather than using the Arawak name *Guanahaní*? Did Columbus have the right to name the Arawaks "Indians"?

have been friendly. They used sign language to communicate and exchanged gifts. Columbus stated that although the villagers had "very keen intelligence," their gentle natures would make it possible for fifty armed men to bring them "under control and made to do whatever one might wish." Then in a forewarning of events to come, Columbus wrote, "Christendom will do good business with these Indians, especially Spain, whose subjects they must all become."

THROUGH ARTISTS' EYES

This painting shows how its artist imagined a meeting between Columbus and the Indians on the islands he visited. Most of the pictures we have of early encounters between Europeans and Indians were painted by European or European-American artists who lived many years after 1492. They painted their pictures from written reports of the explorers or from their own imaginations. Compare this picture with the description of the Indians Columbus wrote in his log.

Having not seen Indians, some European artists depicted Indians as primitive but noble human beings. However, other artists painted images of fierce, brutal savages.

If we had an Indian artist's painting of this same meeting, it might be quite different. Imagine yourself an Arawak artist and draw the meeting from your Indian viewpoint.

Exploring Beyond San Salvador

Although interested in the Arawaks, Columbus was eager to find the Indies mainland. After two days exploring their landing point, Columbus and some of the sailors set off in rowboats to see the rest of the island. In later days, they returned to their ships and sailed to other nearby islands.

Each day Columbus and his crew saw new plants, animals, and often people, most of whom were peaceful and friendly. They found nothing they believed to be of much value—no spices, no gems, and only some traces of gold.

On Christmas Day, 1492, the *Santa María* ran aground and sank off an island some 300 miles south of San Salvador. Unharmed, the captain and his ship's crew moved

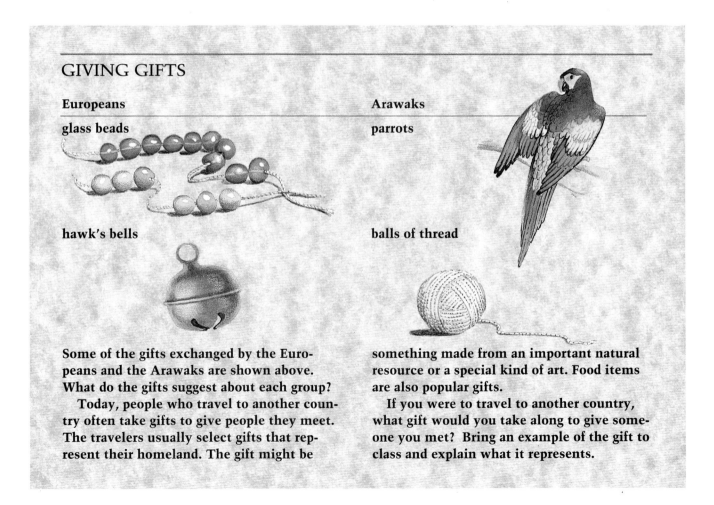

GIVING GIFTS

Europeans

glass beads

hawk's bells

Arawaks

parrots

balls of thread

Some of the gifts exchanged by the Europeans and the Arawaks are shown above. What do the gifts suggest about each group?

Today, people who travel to another country often take gifts to give people they meet. The travelers usually select gifts that represent their homeland. The gift might be something made from an important natural resource or a special kind of art. Food items are also popular gifts.

If you were to travel to another country, what gift would you take along to give someone you met? Bring an example of the gift to class and explain what it represents.

aboard the *Niña* before venturing onto the nearby island. Columbus named this island *Hispaniola,* or "Little Spain," and then directed sailors to build a fort on the island from the wood of the *Santa María.* When the fort was completed, 39 sailors were selected to stay at the fort to protect it.

On January 16, 1493, Columbus and the other sailors set sail for Spain, promising to return to the fort as soon as possible. After they left, all 39 men died. Although the foreigners were probably killed by islanders, the reason for their death remains a mystery. Columbus would not learn that his first attempt to establish a settlement had failed until he returned several months later.

Never the Same Again

As the *Pinta* and *Niña* sailed east toward Spain, Columbus looked forward to reporting his discovery of a new route to

COMMUNICATING WITHOUT WORDS

The Europeans did not speak the Arawaks' language. The Arawaks did not speak the Europeans' language. Yet throughout his travels among the islands, Columbus tried to learn from the islanders where he could find gold, silver, pearls, spices, great cities, and wealthy kings. Each group of islanders he talked to told him that such wealth and people could be found on another island farther away.

Perhaps the islanders did not understand what Columbus was asking. Perhaps they were just being

polite. Maybe they purposefully misled Columbus. Whatever the reasons, Columbus did not learn from the islanders what he wished to know.

With a friend, imagine yourselves as a European and an Arawak. As a European, try communicating your wish to find riches. As an Arawak, try to answer the European's questions and to ask questions of your own. Use hand signals, other body motions, drawings, real objects—anything you can think of—to communicate with your friend.

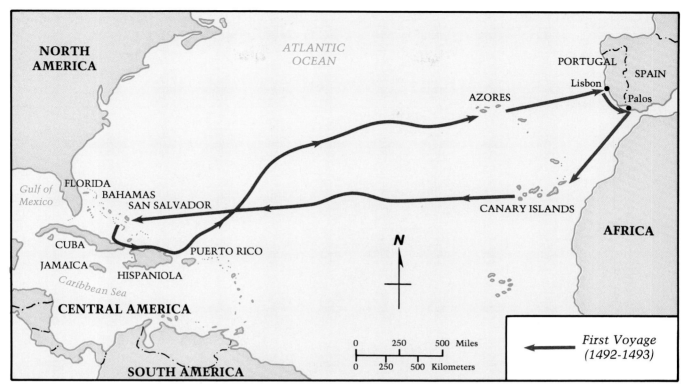

The First Voyage of Columbus, 1492–1493

the Indies. He was disappointed to have little gold and silver aboard the ships, but he felt sure such riches were within reach on a return trip. He was also certain that the people of Spain would be impressed with the exotic birds, plants, and six "Indians" he had kidnapped to bring back as souvenirs.

Columbus did not know that rather than finding a gateway to the Indies, he had bumped into islands that are part of the Bahamas chain. The Bahamas lie between the Atlantic Ocean and Caribbean Sea, south of present-day Florida. These islands would serve as stepping stones for later explorers to reach two continents—North America and South America—previously unknown to Europeans.

With Columbus's ships out of sight and no remaining Europeans on their land, the Arawaks on San Salvador (Guanahaní) returned to their normal activities. They may have thought the Europeans were gods who rose from the sea and then went back to it. They probably thought that their brief encounter with fair-skinned strangers was over.

What neither the Arawaks nor the Europeans knew was how drastically Columbus's visit would change their lives—and the course of world history—in only a few years.

Where Did Columbus Land?
Some navigational information in Columbus's rewritten log is contradictory. Over the years, different interpretations of the log have caused experts to disagree about which island in the Bahamas was the one on which Columbus first landed. Today, most believe his first landfall was on the island we presently call San Salvador.

2

TWO OLD WORLDS
On the Eve of Exchange

When Columbus returned from the Americas to Europe, news of his voyage spread quickly. Some other navigators doubted that Columbus had reached the Indies, but he convinced Queen Isabella and King Ferdinand that his explorations had been successful. Based on the captain's promise to find more gold, they provided money for a second trip.

Opposite page: Picture story about the Aztecs' migration to the lakes of central Mexico, where they founded the city of Tenochtitlán.

Return Trips

In September 1493, Columbus's second expedition landed on Hispaniola with seventeen ships and a crew of 1,200. Loaded on the ships were plants and animals common in Europe. By planting seeds and cuttings, Columbus's crew introduced into the Americas wheat, melons, onions, lettuce, grapes, and sugarcane. The animals they added included horses, pigs, cattle, chickens, sheep, goats, and, accidentally, rats.

Most of the European plants did not thrive well in the tropical islands, although later the same crops would grow successfully in other areas of the Americas. The animals did very well. Having no animal-killing diseases and endless natural feed, the Caribbean islands were an ideal environment for livestock. Within thirty years, the herds had multiplied many times over.

Columbus's crew also gave the Americas an unwelcome gift—disease. Contagious diseases were common in Europe, but the native populations of the Americas had never been exposed to the European diseases. From Columbus's men, Hispaniola islanders caught a lung disease that killed hundreds. In coming years, millions of Indians would die from disease.

Over an eleven-year period, Columbus led four voyages to the Caribbean. During these trips, his crews explored more islands and may have reached the coasts of South and Central America. Columbus continued to claim for Spain the lands he visited and to enslave native people. He searched for gold but never found it in large amounts. Nor was he able to found a lasting *colony*, or settlement.

Although he had discovered a good sailing route from Europe to the Caribbean, Columbus had underestimated the circumference of the earth and overestimated the size of Asia. These errors led him to continue claiming he had reached the Indies. However, other European explorers realized it was not the Indies Columbus had encountered, but a landmass previously unknown to them.

Even before Columbus's final voyage, other navigators were sailing across the Atlantic. In the twelve years after 1492, more than eighty exploration voyages reached the Americas. As these explorers' reports made news, Columbus was nearly forgotten. The lands he first explored for Europe were named not for him but for Amerigo Vespucci, one of the adventurers who followed him. In a famous letter, Vespucci wrote in vivid detail about a *Mundus Novus*, which means a New World.

CULTURAL BORROWING

Caribbean Indians learned about new plants and animals from Columbus's crew, but the Europeans also learned from the islanders. When the sailors saw an Indian product or way of life that would improve their lives, they quickly borrowed the idea.

Sleeping was one unpleasant part of ship-board life. Provided no beds, the sailors slept on the ship's deck. The rolling sea not only kept them tossing about all night, but waves splashing on board soaked them.

On the island of Cuba, Columbus's crew took a special interest in the islanders' beds. Called *hamacas* by the Indians, the beds were woven mats tied between two trees or poles. The sailors soon started using hamacas as their shipboard beds.

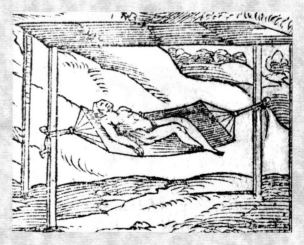

Write an advertisement to describe the advantages of sleeping in a hamaca rather than on a ship deck. What present-day word do we use for hamaca?

The Europeans were able to navigate oceans because of instruments such as the astrolabe (left) and compass (right). The astrolabe was a mechanical model of the movement of the sun, moon, and planets. The compass contained an iron needle that always pointed north and south.

Another Old World

Europeans in 1492 did not know about the American continents. However, ancestors of the people Columbus met had been in the Americas for at least 13,000 years, maybe much longer. From the time of the earth's formation over four billion years ago until the Ice Ages, there were no human residents in the Americas. During the Ice Ages, vast sheets of ice covered much of what is now Canada and the northern United States. These ice sheets froze water in the Bering Sea between northeastern Asia and present-day Alaska.

While the water was frozen, a land bridge existed between Asia and North America. Animals crossed the land bridge between the continents. Scientists believe bands of human hunters from Asia followed large game animals, such as mammoths, mastodons, and bison, across the land bridge. For over 3,000 years, this land bridge allowed small groups of people to pass onto the North American continent.

The people who entered the Americas explored farther and farther south. They traveled down an ice-free path in west central Canada to warmer lands in the northern plains of the United States. From there some went east and others west. Some continued to travel south until they reached Tierra del Fuego, the southern tip of South America.

Rewriting History
Until recently, known evidence of human beings in the Americas was 11,500 years old. Then an American anthropologist, Tom Dillehay, found in Chile, South America, a human footprint that was 13,000 years old. It is the oldest evidence found so far of humans living in the Americas. Some scientists think future findings may prove humans have lived in the Americas even longer than 13,000 years.

Early arrivals in the Americas faced a landscape much like this Alaskan tundra.

Then about 10,000 years ago the Ice Ages ended. The glaciers melted, flooding the land bridge, and migration from Asia across the bridge largely stopped.

A World of Differences

Long after migrants stopped arriving from Asia, the people already in the Americas continued to explore and settle in new locations. As they chose places to make their homes, they adapted to the continents' many different landforms and climates.

Those who settled in colder climates sewed warm, waterproof clothes from the skin of reindeer and seals. Groups who chose desert climates developed ways to store water and irrigate crops. Those living along coastlines became expert fishers. Settlers in high, steep mountains found ways to farm the hillsides. Plains dwellers perfected the skill of hunting buffalo on foot.

The homes of individual groups varied from log houses and cliff caves to buffalo-hide tepees. Groups had their own languages and religions. They also had special forms of art, ceremonies, storytelling, and healing.

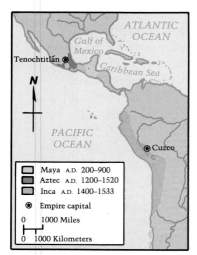

The Three Major Empires in the Americas Before Europeans Arrived

The Indian groups varied in their ways of life. Some were *nomadic,* or roving. Like their ancestors, they hunted wild game and gathered nuts, grains, and fruits. By contrast, other groups had developed farming methods, some quite advanced. These farming people did not move around but instead lived in villages and tended their nearby crop fields.

In Mexico and Central America and along the western coast of South America were three highly developed civilizations. The Aztecs ruled in present-day Mexico. Central America was home to the Mayas, and the Incas controlled western South America. Although the Mayan civilization was declining in 1492, the Aztecs and Incas were expanding theirs. Within their empires were large cities and governments as sophisticated as those in Europe. Their farming methods were among the most advanced in the world.

LEARNING FROM ANCIENT BALL COURTS

Throughout Mexico and Central America are outdoor ball courts where Indians played a ball game using a solid rubber ball somewhat smaller than a soccer ball. The team game required players to keep the ball in the air by using only their hips, knees, and head.

Most ball courts were built of stones in a **T** or **I** shape. High walls formed the sides of the playing area. Spectators watched from stairstep seats on the ends of the stadium.

Similarities among the courts tell anthropologists

A Mayan ball court.

that Indian groups in a large area of the Americas had contact with each other long before 1492. They believe groups learned about the game through visits with each other. Anthropologists study Indian drawings, later writings of the Spanish who saw the game being played, and the courts themselves to trace the game's spread across the Americas.

Draw a picture of your favorite outdoor game's playing area. Without naming the game, ask a classmate to identify it.

The Aztecs and Incas sent traders out to find, trade with, and report on people beyond their empires. In addition, most of the smaller farming and nomadic groups had some contact with other Indian groups. From their contacts, the groups exchanged ideas about hunting, farming, art, and daily life.

None of the Indians' previous contacts with each other prepared them for their encounters with the uninvited Europeans who arrived on their shores. Aided by horses, metal weapons, disease, and broken promises, the Europeans would invade every corner of the two continents over the next 400 years. Millions of Indians would lose their lands and their lives. Indian history and ways of living would be nearly destroyed. The story of the European invasion of the Americas is a story not of discovery but of conquest.

THE MAJESTIC AZTECS

In the valley where Mexico City now stands, the Aztecs built their empire's twin capital cities, Tenochtitlán-Tlatelolco, in the early 1300s. The cities' pyramids, palaces, floating gardens, canals, and zoos prompted the first European visitors to declare them "a wonderful thing to behold."

Aztec rulers had been quite successful in expanding their lands. Often using military might, the Aztecs forced people they conquered to pay tribute, or taxes, in the form of crops, goods, and slaves. Food and goods were stored in warehouses for use by the rulers or sold in the capitals' huge markets.

If the Europeans had not defeated the Aztecs, the Aztecs might have extended their empire to what is now the United States. Draw your community as it might look today if it were part of the Aztec empire.

The Great Temple of Tenochtitlán.

God, Gold, and Glory

The Spanish adventurers who followed Columbus to the Americas were called *conquistadors,* the Spanish word for conquerors. The conquistadors had three purposes. One purpose was to convince the people they met to accept their God and their religion, Christianity. Another was to find gold, silver, and other precious metals that would make them wealthy in Europe. Finally, the explorers wanted to become famous by claiming lands and establishing colonies.

Driven by their quest for God, gold, and glory, few of the first Europeans made an effort to understand either the land or the people of the Americas. Instead, they formed many inaccurate ideas about the Indians and their lands. These false ideas, or myths, were planted in the minds of many Europeans. Some were believed for centuries.

THE IMPERIAL INCAS

At about the same time as the Aztecs, the Incas were building their civilization high in the Andes mountains of present-day Peru. From their capital city of Cuzco, the Incas began to expand their empire by conquering people beyond their borders. Once conquered, local people had to pay tribute to the Inca rulers.

To keep their huge empire working, the Inca rulers directed the building of a vast road system, totaling some 25,000 miles. They also developed a tool for counting and for keeping track of the tribute owed them. Called a *quipu,* the abacus-like device was made of cords of different colors knotted in specific ways to show various numbers of items.

With a partner, make a quipu and create a system for knotting the cords to count numbers up to 1,000.

This cliff dwelling is an example of Anasazi Indian architecture in what is now the southwestern United States. The Anasazi culture existed from about A.D. 350 to 1300.

The Lure of Gold

For centuries, land had been Europe's measure of wealth. Only a few people owned land. In the late 1400s, gold and silver began to be accepted as standards of wealth. In time these precious metals replaced land as the basis of Europe's economy. Individuals who had gold and silver were considered wealthy. Countries with these riches became powerful.

Myths about the Americas

Perhaps the first myth about the Americas was in the name *New World*. Land in the Americas was the same age as the rest of the earth. People had been settled throughout the two continents for at least 10,000 years. The Americas were new only to the Europeans.

Another myth credited the Europeans with "discovering" America, yet the Indians had explored nearly all the land of the two vast continents thousands of years before. They also had discovered many natural treasures, including gold and silver.

Many of the early explorers called the Americas "unsettled," but Indian groups lived on most of the habitable land in both North and South America. Settlement to the Indians, especially the nomadic groups, was different from settlement to the Europeans. Most Indians did not claim to own land; they merely used the land. By contrast, nearly all European land was owned by individuals in 1492. Europe, a small continent, was crowded. Farmers had worn out much of their land and needed new soil to feed the continent's population. To most explorers, the Americas seemed to offer unlimited free land, and they did not hesitate to settle in the homelands of Indians.

Because they did not see certain examples of European civilization, some early explorers spread the myth that people in the Americas were "primitive" and "uncivilized." They pointed out that Indians did not have complete written languages or printing presses to publish books. Nor had they developed technology for making objects such as guns and metal tools. Because some large animals had become extinct in the Americas at the end of the Ice Age, Indians did not have beasts such as horses and oxen for carrying people and heavy objects.

Although Indians who lived near bodies of water were skillful sailors, they did not have navigation equipment, like the compass, needed to sail across the oceans. The Europeans' navigation instruments had allowed them to

Historians believe the design on this bison-hide Sioux Indian shield shows the clash between Indians and Europeans.

THE BISON HUNT

For thousands of years, North American Indians hunted bison, an ancestor of the buffalo, with the "stampede and jump" method. Hunters guided a herd of bison toward a ravine, then stampeded them over the edge. Animals that didn't die from the fall were killed with spears, and some were butchered.

The development of bows and arrows gradually changed North American Indian hunting methods. More drastic changes occurred after Europeans introduced Indians to horses and guns.

Anthropologists estimate that each day early Indian adult males ate more than ten pounds of fresh meat. That's more than forty quarter-pound hamburgers! Why do you think Indian hunters ate so much more meat than most present-day adult men?

explore beyond their continent, especially the western coast of Africa and islands in the Atlantic Ocean.

Europe was divided into many small countries that were ruled by kings and queens and were often at war with one another. Other than the Aztec and Inca empires, Indians had not divided their continents into "countries." Many foreigners considered tribal governments primitive. They also judged the Indians' nature-centered religions to be inferior to their own more "civilized" Christian religion.

Looking Back at the Americas in 1492

Most Europeans did not recognize, and we are now only beginning to fully understand, the accomplishments of many Indian groups 500 years ago. For example, the Aztecs were able to build their huge pyramids and buildings because of their knowledge of mathematics and physics. Indian solar calendars were more accurate than European calendars.

INUIT CONSERVATION

Far north in the Arctic, where for weeks in the winter the sun doesn't rise, live the Inuits. For thousands of years they have survived one of the world's harshest climates.

In 1982, scientists uncovered a 500-year-old Inuit home that had been frozen in time when a sudden surge of sea ice buried it. Inside, perfectly preserved, were its dwellers and all their possessions. Studying this remarkable find, anthropologists learned that the ancient Inuits used every part of the animals they hunted—skin for kayaks and sleds, bones and horns for tools, meat for eating, and blubber for heating.

The Inuits did not waste their wildlife resources. Describe one way in which you avoid wasting a natural resource.

These present-day White Mountain Apaches of Arizona are climbing up Sacred Mountain to give thanks for the land.

Careful recording of weather patterns and soil conditions helped Indian farmers successfully grow a wide variety of plants in a broad range of climates and soils. By crossing plants growing in the wild, Indians created new crops. They also developed natural medicines from plants to control diseases and treat many illnesses.

The Indians' traditions of family and community life were also remarkable. Most had strong family ties, with parents and grandparents serving as childrens' teachers. Family and community histories were passed down through story-telling and through drawings on cave walls, hides, pottery, and woven cloth.

Today, we especially admire the Indians' knowledge of and respect for nature. Present-day scientists are trying to relearn what many Indians 500 years ago already knew about conserving the land and resources of our planet.

Columbus's accidental landing in the Americas did not fulfill his dreams, but it did bring two long-separated areas together. The encounter set off the most important plant, animal, disease, and cultural exchanges in all history. In the next five chapters, you will learn how five "seeds of change" were planted 500 years ago with the Columbus voyages and continue to influence the lives of people throughout the world today.

The League of Iroquois
The Iroquois, a group of five Indian tribes, lived in what is now the northeast United States. Perhaps as early as 1450, the tribes began to unite against their enemies. With a sixth tribe, they had formed a league by the early 1700s. Framers of the U.S. Constitution studied the Iroquois League as one model for uniting the thirteen colonies.

The Iroquois used beaded wampum belts to record important events. This one records a treaty.

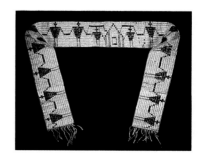

25

3 DEVASTATING DISEASE
An Invisible Enemy

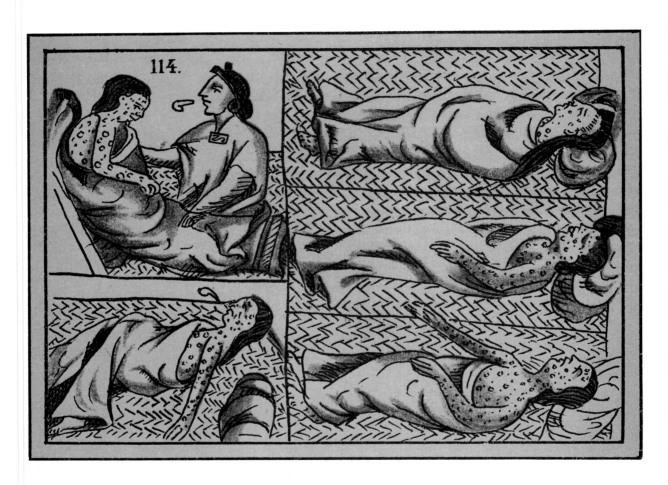

Do you remember getting ready for your first day of kindergarten? You may have bought school supplies or some new clothes. You probably visited your doctor or a clinic where you were given a vaccine to protect you against diseases. A *vaccine* is medicine that keeps people from getting an infectious disease. *Infectious diseases* are those that spread from person to person, usually through the air or by human touch.

In 1492, there were no vaccines. When the Europeans came to the Americas, they brought several infectious diseases with them. One disease, smallpox, proved to be the most deadly enemy of North and South American Indians— more deadly than all the Europeans' guns.

Europe's Long History with Diseases

If you had been born in Europe 500 years ago, you would have had only one chance in two of living to age fifteen. So many children died from measles, typhus, diphtheria, yellow fever, smallpox, and other infectious diseases that they were called "childhood diseases," a term we still use today.

People who survived childhood developed an immunity to the common European diseases. *Immunity* is a condition of the body that keeps it from being infected by a certain disease. For many years before they began coming to the Americas, European adventurers had traveled to Africa and Asia, where they were exposed to diseases common on those continents. The travelers brought these diseases back to Europe, often causing epidemics. An *epidemic* is the rapid spread of a particular infectious disease among many people. Through years of epidemics, Europeans had built up immunities to a wide range of infectious diseases.

The Isolated Americas

The story of disease in the Americas begins with the Bering land bridge migrants, at least 13,000 years before Columbus's landing. Although no one knows for sure, the migrants into the Americas may have carried with them diseases from Asia. However, those who were seriously ill

Opposite page: An Aztec story picture, called a codex, *shows stages of smallpox infection.*

Dreaded Smallpox
Smallpox was passed through the air, human touch, and contact with infected objects. The first symptoms were aches, fever, and vomiting. Then a rash of small pimples soon grew larger and filled with pus. For those who survived, scabs fell off in about a month, leaving most with scars. In 1796, Edward Jenner, an English doctor, developed the world's first vaccine: a vaccine against smallpox. By 1980, smallpox had been eliminated everywhere in the world.

from the diseases probably did not survive the cold climate of the Arctic.

The small bands who settled the American continents seem to have had few infectious diseases. Most lived in small communities and had limited contacts with outsiders. The continents were not free of diseases, but the groups' isolation kept them generally healthy. Their isolation also kept them from building up immunities to infectious diseases.

Throughout the Americas, Indians successfully used plants and herbs to treat illnesses. Although European doctors also used plant medicines, Indian healers were more advanced in their knowledge of plants. For example, Aztec doctors had recorded more than 1,200 plants that aided in the treatment of specific illnesses.

European Diseases Arrive

All the Indians' medical knowledge did not prepare them for the invisible enemy: disease brought by Europeans. Some of the Arawaks who first met Columbus caught a lung disease

HEALTH PROFILE OF AN AZTEC WARRIOR

The Spanish conquistadors were impressed with the physical bodies and health of the Aztec people. One conquistador wrote, "The people of this land are well made, rather tall than short. They are swarthy as leopards . . . skillful, robust, and tireless."

The Aztecs practiced good health habits. They bathed regularly in streams and lakes. Homes in the cities had bathhouses in which family members took steambaths both to clean themselves and to treat coughs, fevers, and sore joints. The Aztecs cleaned their teeth often with powdered charcoal and salt.

Many Aztec healers were specialists in particular illnesses. Herbal medicines were commonly used to treat patients.

List five things present-day people do to try to keep themselves healthy.

from his sailors and died. However, it was not until 1518 that the full force of disease first struck the Americas. Gonzalo Fernández de Oviedo y Valdés, an early Spanish historian of the Americas, wrote that a highly infectious disease, probably smallpox, struck the island of Hispaniola, where the Spanish had started their first permanent colony.

Oviedo estimated that a million Indians lived on Hispaniola in 1518. Thirty years later, fewer than 1,000 Indians had survived the disease. From Hispaniola, the smallpox epidemic spread, probably through Indian traders, to other islands in the Caribbean as well as into areas of present-day Mexico, Central America, and perhaps Peru.

Historians think the smallpox epidemic may have started when a few smallpox scabs got into a bundle of rags on one of the explorer ships. Later, the scabs found their way to the islanders. Perhaps one or more sailors left Europe infected with the disease and broke out with the pox after arriving in the Caribbean.

In coming years, epidemic after epidemic of European

HEALTH PROFILE OF A SPANISH CONQUISTADOR

Most Spanish conquistadors were tough and wiry men who had survived exposure to childhood diseases. Many had pockmarks on their bodies, evidence of their earlier bouts with smallpox. They also had survived the crowded and unclean living conditions of most European cities in which open garbage dumps and bacteria-infected water supplies were common.

Generally, conquistadors did not practice good health habits. They seldom bathed or brushed their teeth, and they did not have a nutritious diet.

If a conquistador fell ill during his travels, he was treated by a barber-surgeon who both cut hair and treated medical problems.

List four conditions described in the conquistador's profile that today we know can lead to sickness and disease.

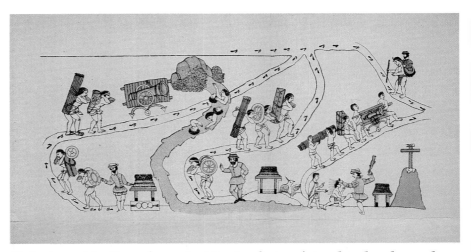

Painting of Indian slaves in Mexico being forced to haul supplies for Cortés.

An Inca Medicine

Some early European explorers brought with them malaria, a disease unknown in the Americas before 1492. Causing chills and high fever, malaria is spread by mosquitoes. The disease became epidemic in swampy and humid areas where mosquitoes thrive.

Incas had long used the bark from the cinchona tree, which grew in the Andes, to cure cramps, chills, and fevers. European explorers began to use cinchona to produce quinine, which helped prevent malaria attacks. Without quinine to treat malaria, European settlement of humid regions in the Americas might not have been possible.

diseases swept through the Caribbean and onto the mainlands wherever Indians had contact with Europeans or other infected Indians. The diseases were made worse by the often brutal treatment of the Indians enslaved by the Europeans. Together, diseases and enslavement killed millions of native people in the Americas.

Some Indians tried to get revenge by infecting the Europeans' food and water with the blood of diseased Indians. The Indians' efforts had little effect because most Europeans had immunity to the diseases. The grief of one Indian is expressed in this description of his people before the arrival of the Europeans.

> *There was then no sickness; they had no aching bones, they had no high fever, they had then no smallpox; they had then no burning chest; they had then no abdominal pain; they had then no consumption; they had then no headache. At that time the course of humanity was orderly. The foreigners made it otherwise when they arrived here.*

The Beginning of Mainland Conquest

Disease spread through the Caribbean as Spanish conquistadors (conquerors) moved onto the mainlands of North and South America. One early conquistador to arrive on the mainland was Hernán Cortés. In 1519, with pigs and horses from the Caribbean, Cortés set sail for the continents. With him traveled 550 conquistadors and 200 Caribbean Indians whom he had enslaved. The group landed on the eastern coast of what is now Mexico. The Indians who discovered Cortés led him and his group from the coast to the Aztec capital, Tenochtitlán.

The conquistadors were not the first outsiders to visit the Aztec capital and Montezuma II, the Aztec leader. However, these visitors with their fair skin, European clothing, armor, guns, and horses were different. An Aztec legend predicted that an ancient god, Quetzalcoatl, would one day return to Tenochtitlán to take back his kingdom. Perhaps Montezuma believed Cortés was Quetzalcoatl.

Hoping to persuade the visitors to leave his land, Montezuma offered Cortés gifts of gold, silver, and jade. The treasures convinced the Spanish to conquer the Aztecs and enslave them to mine the precious metals. Realizing Cortés's plan, the Aztecs prepared to defend their empire.

DISEASE IN ART

Although most Indian groups in the Americas did not have a written language, some left information about their health in various art forms. Paintings on skins, rocks, and cloth were used by some groups. Others included health information in their oral stories and ceremonies.

One group, the Moche of Peru, who lived before the Incas, made detailed pottery figures. Their figures show various medical problems such as missing arms and legs, skin diseases, blindness, cleft palate, and misformed feet. The figure here shows a woman with a disease that caused her lips and nose to rot. This disease still affects some people in parts of Peru and Brazil.

Draw a picture of a vase. On it illustrate an illness or medical problem you have had.

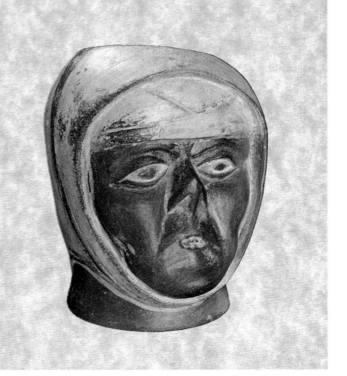

When the battle began, Cortés's force of 750 faced more than a million Aztecs. After two years, the Aztec lands lay in ruins, thousands of Aztecs were dead, and the empire was ruled by the Spanish. How could this have happened?

Although horses and guns gave the Spanish an advantage, smallpox turned out to be the Aztecs' worst enemy. Historians believe that a smallpox epidemic in the Aztec empire was started by one Spanish soldier who was infected with the disease. Housed with an Aztec family, the soldier infected members of that family, who in turn infected their neighbors. The disease spread like wildfire, and the Aztec empire was soon conquered. It was the first of many European conquests in the Americas.

The Spread of Disease

After its introduction into the Americas, smallpox often spread on its own. From the Caribbean islands and Central

IF BONES COULD TALK

Anthropologists dig up and study human bones that have been buried for hundreds of years. They learn, among other things, about the health of the people buried.

As the scientists start to dig, they are careful to look at the way in which the bones are buried. Bones of many different bodies in one grave are a clue that a disease epidemic might have hit the community and caused many deaths at the same time.

Scientists often take the bones to laboratories to look for signs of how people died. Were they killed with bullets or arrows? Did they die of a disease that affected the bones? Did they die from unsuccessful medical treatments such as surgery?

Some Indian groups object to having their ancestors' bones removed from their graves

for study. With classmates, discuss the conflict between scientists' search for new knowledge about the past and Indians' respect for their ancestors. List possible ways to resolve the conflict.

Drawings by a Sioux Indian artist on a cotton cloth record major events in the tribe's life from 1798 to 1902. In this detail, two smallpox epidemics are each represented by an image of a person covered with pox. Can you find the images?

America, diseases, particularly smallpox, traveled along the Indian trade routes established before 1492. Probably the diseases were carried by both the traders and their goods.

When diseases came to Indian communities ahead of the Europeans, the work of the conquerors was much easier. Francisco Pizarro led his conquistadors into South America to conquer the Inca empire in 1531. When he arrived, he discovered that the Incas' great leader, Huayna Capac, his captains, and thousands of Inca people had died—all with "their faces covered with scabs." The remaining people were fighting among themselves for control of the empire. By 1533, Pizarro and his soldiers had overtaken the mighty Incas.

Smallpox also spread north into what is now the United States and Canada. English, French, and Spanish explorers reported in their journals about coming upon empty Indian villages where only the bodies of the dead remained.

In the northern plains of the United States, smallpox appeared years before the first Europeans arrived. The disease spread from tribe to tribe through trade and wars. In 1781,

Old History— New Understandings
Diseases brought by Europeans were "more deadly than sword and gunpowder," said historian P. M. Ashburn. He wrote these words in his 1947 book, *The Ranks of Death*. The book caused readers to reconsider just how important disease had been in the Europeans' conquest of the Americas. Our understanding of history is often changed by new information.

Facial scars show that Running Face, a Mandan Indian, survived the smallpox epidemic of 1837 that killed most of his people.

Blackfoot Indian scouts came upon a Shoshone tribe's village. The village was silent, and no people were visible. Careful to avoid a trap, the scouts entered the village quietly, only to discover all the people dead in their tepees. Overjoyed with their luck, the scouts looted the camp and returned home with the Shoshones' possessions. Within weeks, as many as two thirds of the Blackfoot tribe were dying from the smallpox that had infected the Shoshones' belongings.

Infectious disease had its worst impact in the first 100 years after the Europeans' arrival. Some groups, such as the Arawaks, were almost completely destroyed. Other groups had more survivors, but their numbers were greatly reduced. Although less frequent after the 1500s, epidemics continued. Experts estimate that disease killed 50 to 90 percent of North America's Indians between 1500 and 1900.

The Never-Ending Story of Disease

Of all the changes set off by the arrival of Europeans in the Americas, none was faster, more widespread, or more deadly than the introduction of disease—especially smallpox. Massive epidemics were not controlled until after 1800,

POPULATION CHANGES

From 1492 to 1900 the Indian population of the Americas dropped by as much as 90 percent. Indians died from warfare, forced migration, and especially disease. During the same period, the number of native peoples in Europe, Asia, and Africa greatly increased. Corn and potatoes, new food crops from the Americas, were largely responsible for this huge growth.

    Study the graph to compare how the meeting of two old worlds affected the population of four continents.

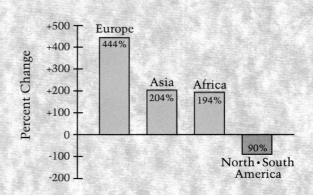

Percent Change in Native Populations by Continent, 1492–1900

when the smallpox vaccine began to be widely used and vaccines for other diseases also became available. A few infectious diseases had their origin in the Americas. However, none has led to massive epidemics on other continents.

Unfortunately, infectious disease is still with us. Since 1980, AIDS, Acquired Immune Deficiency Syndrome, has become a worldwide epidemic. Although AIDS does not spread through the air as smallpox did, it has killed thousands each year.

The people of the Americas in 1492 had no way to resist the invisible enemy that brought death to thousands and left the rest weakened and disheartened. As you think about the story of disease in the Americas, consider this question: How might history be different if no disease had traveled with the Europeans and they had met the Indians of the Americas at the Indians' full strength?

NEW VICTIMS OF OLD DISEASES

In the dense rain forests of Venezuela and Brazil, the Yanomamo Indians lived for centuries with little contact from other people. In the past few years, logging and mining companies have built roads into the homelands of the Yanomamo. Workers brought with them old diseases, including measles, influenza, malaria, and chicken pox. The Yanomamo have no immunity to these diseases. Even modern vaccines have not been able to save many of the infected Yanomamos. When medicines fail, the Yanomamo depend on their tribal healer to treat the ill.

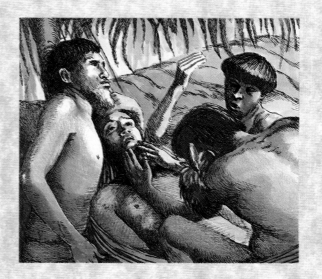

Imagine an infectious disease without a cure striking your country. How would you try to protect yourself and your loved ones against the disease? Should the government take action to prevent an epidemic?

4 AMAZING MAIZE
An Indian Gift to the World

If you were asked to identify the single most important discovery in the history of humankind, what would you name? Fire? The wheel? Electricity? Space travel? Many history experts agree on one answer—the discovery of farming.

A Most Important Discovery

Before humans discovered farming, they had to roam from place to place looking for their next meal. Whether hunting animals or gathering nuts and berries, early humans were always on the move. Then about 7,000 to 10,000 years ago, people began to grow crops and raise animals. In other words, they began to farm.

We are not sure exactly how farming began. It may have happened by accident, when someone tossed some seeds into soft soil and discovered that they grew into plants. We do know that once farming was discovered, human life changed forever. People began to live in villages, and population increased. A surplus food supply allowed villagers time to make artistic objects and to develop leisure activities.

The first farmers probably grew most of their crops by planting seeds from wild grasses or plants. However, one early crop never grew wild. It came about only by the systematic and careful work of early farmers, and it changed the diet of people around the world forever. Today we call their crop corn, but the first farmers called it maize.

Maize in the Americas

Scientists have discovered that the first maize was grown 7,000 years ago about 125 miles southeast of present-day Mexico City, Mexico. Later, maize was grown by the Aztecs, Mayas, and Incas. The map on page 18 shows where the Maya, Aztec, and Inca empires were located. Probably these early farmers crossed the pollen and silk of different wild grasses until they developed a form of maize.

Anthropologists have found preserved examples of maize throughout the Americas. From these, we know different kinds of maize were grown by different peoples.

Opposite page: Modern-day corn harvest.

What's in a Name?
The first Spanish explorers called corn by its Indian name, *mahiz*. Over time this word became *maize*. To later English colonists the word *corn* referred to any grain that could be eaten. They called the grain introduced to them in the Americas *Indian corn*. Today, the word *corn* is used in America and the word *maize* in Europe.

TRAVAXO
3ARA·CALL·CHAIARCVI·PA

Left: Ancient Incas harvesting corn. Right: A modern-day Mayan farmer in a corn field. Compare the traditional farming method shown here with the machine harvest on page 36.

Master Farmers

The Indians' farming methods were as remarkable as their creation of maize. For example, Indian farmers carefully selected the best seeds from each harvest to save for planting the next year's crops. Rather than simply tossing seeds onto the soil, they dug holes and planted the seeds. To nurture their crops, they watered the plants and cleared away weeds. They learned which plants grew well together and intermixed their crops.

Maize became a staple crop of the Mayan, Aztec, and Incan civilizations. From the dry plateaus of central Mexico to the wet lowlands of Guatemala, and from the irrigated fields of coastal Peru to the mountains of Colombia, maize was cultivated. The Indians also developed ways to preserve their crops. Boiling ears of maize and grinding maize kernels into meal were both common ways of preparing the grain.

By 1492, when the first Europeans arrived in the Americas, the knowledge of how to grow maize had spread beyond Central and South America into what is now the United States and Canada. Desert Indians of present-day Arizona and New Mexico cultivated corn. So did Indians along the Missouri and Mississippi rivers and tribes as far north as southern Ontario, Canada. Maize was grown in the southeastern region of the United States over 3,000 years ago.

Maize was so important that each tribe had its own name for it. Some of the names can be translated into English as *Our Mother* or *Our Life,* names suggesting that Indians viewed corn as the very source of life. Some experts believe the great empires of the Americas would never have been built if the Indians had not developed their sophisticated methods of agriculture and a reliable supply of maize to feed their peoples.

In the Hands of Europeans

The first Europeans who landed in the Americas hoped, above all, to find gold and silver. They would have been happy to find spices such as the nutmeg, cloves, and ginger that earlier explorers had brought back to Europe from Asia. These treasures they did not find, at least not in the abundance for which they had hoped. What they did see was maize, growing nearly everywhere. Europeans had never

MALE AND FEMALE CORN?

Each corn plant grows from a seed. Once a seed is planted, a small miracle occurs.

First, the seed develops the corn's root system and stalk, its "trunk" above the ground. Each stalk has a male and female part. The male part, called the *tassel,* is at the top of the stalk and gives off pollen. The pollen attaches itself to the female part, called *silk,* which grows out of the corn ears. When pollen attaches to the silk, the process is called *fertilization.* The fertilized silk then develops kernels on the cob inside the husk.

Corn reaches its full size and ripens about eight weeks after fertilization. Depending on the type of corn, the stalk can grow as high as twenty feet!

With a classmate, measure a height of twenty feet. Can you find other objects of the same height in your environment?

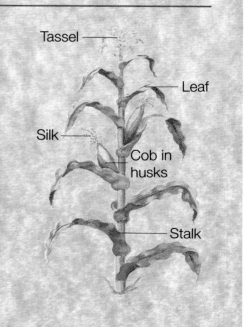

Tassel

Leaf

Silk

Cob in husks

Stalk

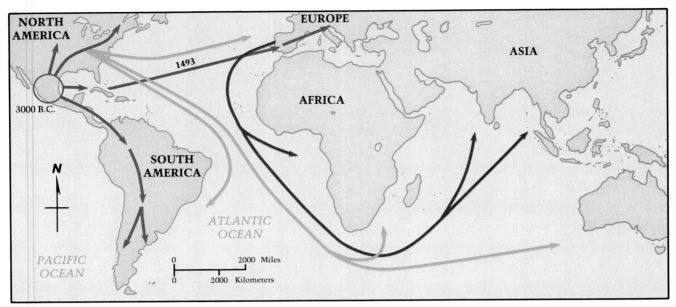

The Spread of Corn from the Americas to the World

seen maize because it did not grow on their continent or in Asia and Africa, where some of them had traveled.

The earliest written reference to corn by a European is in Christopher Columbus's log. After landing on the island of San Salvador, Columbus sent two men to explore what is now Cuba. Based on their reports, Columbus wrote about "a sort of grain they called maiz." Columbus probably introduced maize to Europe on his return trip to Spain.

After its arrival in Europe, maize became a staple crop in Portugal. From there it spread across Europe into southern France, through northern Italy into Yugoslavia, into Romania, and on to Turkey in Asia.

Many historians believe corn was a major cause of population growth in the southern parts of Europe in the 1600s and 1700s. Although farmers learned to grow maize, Europeans in many areas did not develop a taste for it. Instead, much of the grain was used to feed livestock. Maize helped increase the number of cattle and pigs and made the animals a better source of protein for humans. A better food supply allowed Europeans to have larger families.

Modern scientists use the term Zea Mays *to refer to all the kinds of corn grown by Indians.* Zea *means "the cause of life."*

Corn in the Americas after 1492

The Europeans' use of maize in the Americas did not benefit the Indians, maize's first farmers. The conquistadors who marched into the Americas ignored the Indians' farming technology. Instead they sought to force the Indians to help them take back to Europe the gold and silver riches they found. Sadly, the Europeans were greatly aided in their conquests by the Indians' storehouses of grains and other supplies. The conquistadors found and looted these food supplies—enough to feed not only themselves but the Indians they enslaved as well.

In later years, as Europeans began to colonize the Americas, they adopted the Indians' methods of corn growing. You may remember the story of Squanto, the English-speaking Patuxet Indian who helped the Pilgrims. After their 1620 landing at Plymouth (in present-day Massachusetts), the Pilgrims had little food. Squanto taught them how to plant corn and catch fish.

As more European settlers came to North America in the 1700s and 1800s, they were lured westward by the promise of inexpensive land in the present-day states of Illinois, Indiana, Iowa, and Missouri. Farmers who moved to these areas soon learned that when they planted corn, they were nearly assured a harvest. Corn rarely failed. In the midwestern United States, corn became king. News of fertile and cheap corn land spread throughout the world and brought more immigrant farmers, who took over lands once

Pottery figure of Mayan earth god emerging from corn stalk.

DISCOVERING WHAT DID NOT HAPPEN

Like detectives, historians look for clues in stories, poems, and legends to answer questions about specific events or ways of life in past times. They don't always find clues—which can be as helpful as finding them. How can this be? Try to think like a detective as you read these facts:

- Maize is not mentioned in the Bible.
- Greek and Roman writers say nothing about maize.

- Poems and folktales from India do not mention maize.
- Literature from ancient China does not include references to maize.
- The myths of the Mayas, Aztecs, and Incas describe how important maize was in the lives of these people.

Based on the clues, how would you answer these questions: Where did corn begin? Where did corn not begin?

For centuries, women in Mexico have ground corn into cornmeal for making tortillas, or thin pancakes. Early European immigrants adopted the Indian practice of making cornmeal, which they used in breads. Today, many Americans enjoy tortillas and corn chips.

the home of many Indian tribes. Corn helped the newcomers establish themselves in the Americas, just as it had helped the Indians build their civilizations.

Corn in Africa

Before and after Europeans landed in the Americas, they traveled around the Mediterranean Sea and along the coast of Africa. In their travels, they traded with local peoples. Historians know corn was being grown in West Africa by A.D. 1550. They think traders from Turkey had introduced corn to eastern Africa by A.D. 1561.

African farmers welcomed corn as well as many other American crops such as peanuts, squashes, pumpkins, and sweet potatoes. Like the Indians, African farmers intermixed their crops and could easily add new crops to their gardens.

One of the saddest chapters in the history of corn is the role it played in the enslavement of Africans. When Europeans first began to colonize the Americas, they often enslaved local Indians to do the hard labor of developing and working plantations. However, many Indians died from epidemics of European disease. Others refused to become slaves and were killed or ran away. In time, the plantation owners found themselves short of workers. They believed they could solve their labor problems by enslaving Africans, a practice well known in Europe.

Beginning in the 1500s, European slave traders brought African slaves to the Americas. Arriving in Africa with a load of corn and other goods from the Americas, the slavers traded their goods for Africans who had been hunted down and kidnapped. After packing slaves tightly between the narrow decks of the slave ships and chaining them back to back, slavers kept their bounty alive with a diet of corn meal combined with small portions of other foods.

Describing the diet of African captives on his slave ship, one captain wrote:

> *Their chief diet is call'd dabbadabb, being Indian Corn ground as small as oat-meal, in iron mills, which we carry for that purpose; and after mix'd with water and boil'd well in a large copper furnace, till 'tis as thick as pudding.*

In this way, corn, which had great life-giving potential for people in Africa, contributed to the enslavement of many Africans. Despite their cruel treatment, these unwilling

THE HOPI KACHINA CULT

Corn is the most important crop of the Hopi Indians of Arizona. An important part of the Hopi religion is to ask the spirits for water to help their corn grow. The Hopi have created dolls, or *kachinas*, to represent spirits of people, animals, and plants. One of the most popular kachinas is Ka-ë, Corn Dancer, shown in the photo. This kachina represents a Hopi prayer for corn growth.

Study the picture of the kachina to the right. How can you tell that the doll represents a corn spirit?

Choose a food, animal, or object that is important to you. Draw a kachina-type doll to represent it.

This Corn Dancer kachina was created by Hopi wood-carver Von Monongya.

immigrants would help build and greatly enrich the two American continents.

Corn Today and Tomorrow

If you live in Iowa, Illinois, Nebraska, Indiana, or Minnesota, you probably know about the cultivation of corn because many acres of it are grown in your state. These states are located in what is called the *Corn Belt*. However, some corn is grown in nearly every state. The United States produces about 40 percent of all the corn grown in the world. China is the world's second largest corn-producing nation.

Like the early Indians, we like to eat corn. Who hasn't enjoyed the taste of the season's first corn on the cob? We also enjoy corn that is in breakfast cereals, cooked foods like tortillas, and salad dressings. Popped corn is so popular in some areas that specialty stores sell only popcorn—seasoned with a variety of flavors.

BLUE CORN FOR STARVING PEOPLE

Scientists in Santa Fe, New Mexico, are trying to discover how the Hopi Indians of Arizona developed a special corn two hundred years ago. The corn grown by the Hopis, called blue corn, grows an eighteen-inch cob. It grows low to the ground, with shorter stalks and fewer leaves than most corn. The energy and water saved is channeled into the cob. The researchers are also studying the Hopis' red, pink, and turquiose varieties.

Scientists are interested in the Hopi blue corn and in the Hopi method of cultivation because the corn grows so well in the desert areas of the southwestern United States. They think this corn may be able to grow in Ethiopia, a mostly desert country with millions of starving people.

Use a classroom atlas to find the desert areas of the world. In addition to Ethiopia, what other countries might be helped by Hopi blue corn?

Ethanol reduces air pollution by cutting the amount of carbon released into the air by cars.

In spite of all the corn products on our tables, only about fifteen of every hundred bushels of corn grown in the United States are eaten by people. What happens to the rest? A large amount of it is used to feed farm livestock such as hogs, cattle, chickens, and turkeys. Because humans eat these animals and their products, corn feeds us indirectly through the animals.

We now use corn in ways its first farmers would never have imagined. For example, did you know that corn is used to make explosives, paints, and drugs? How about paper products and textiles? If we were to name all the modern-day products that come from corn, our list would have more than 1,000 items!

A recent development that holds great promise for the future is the use of corn as a fuel for cars and trucks. Corn is processed into a fuel called *ethanol,* which is blended with gasoline. Experts believe ethanol will help reduce our need for oil, a resource that cannot be renewed. In the future, we may use corn starch pellets as packing material. The pellets, which look like plastic foam "popcorn," dissolve in water and are safe for the environment.

For thousands of years, Indians of the Americas have respected the value of corn. Only 500 years ago this simple food grain left the shores of the Americas to begin its journey around the world. Today this gift from the Indians is shared by people worldwide. Maize is truly amazing!

Corn starch packing pellets.

45

Imagine you could choose only one food to eat for the rest of your life. Which food would you choose? Some experts say the potato would be your best choice. It provides a good combination of vitamins, minerals, and fiber. Potatoes have no fat and are nearly salt free. A diet of whole milk and potatoes supplies almost all the nutrition humans need to keep their bodies healthy. No wonder so many people throughout the world eat potatoes!

The potato is a vegetable. A *vegetable* is a nutritious food that comes from the leaves, roots, seeds, or stems of certain plants. A potato is actually the storage stem of a potato plant. The storage stem of a plant is called a *tuber*.

If someone sent you to a garden to bring home potatoes, how would you find them among the other crops? First, you would look for a green plant with leafy stems and white flowers. You would not see potatoes above ground. To get to the potatoes, you would have to dig beneath the plant to find its tubers. There you would see three or more potatoes. These are the only part of the potato plant that can be eaten.

At the time of the first Columbus voyage, the Incas living high in the Andes Mountains of South America had developed ways to grow the not-so-pretty potato. How did the potato get from the Andes to the tables of families around the world? The story that follows tells how this Inca crop became a powerful seed of change.

Where Potatoes First Grew

The potato's history began in the Andes Mountains. The Andes lie along the Pacific Ocean side of South America. This craggy mountain range—the world's longest—runs north to south for almost 4,500 miles from Panama to the southern tip of Chile. The Andes climate is one of great contrasts. It ranges from very warm to very cold and can change rapidly.

Located in the central part of the Andes, in Peru and western Bolivia, is Lake Titicaca. At an elevation of 12,507 feet, Lake Titicaca is the world's highest lake. Scientists

Opposite page: Modern-day potato products.

Planting Potatoes
To plant potatoes, a farmer cuts a potato into large pieces, making sure each piece has an "eye." The eye contains tiny buds that become stems for new plants. In about 100 days, with regular watering, one plant will produce between three and twenty potatoes.

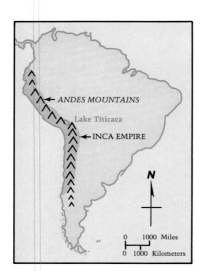

The Inca Empire in South America

Stone walls supported the Incas' terraced fields. The walls helped stop the soil from washing away in heavy rains.

A Riddle

Four people had been stranded on an island for a year when rescuers found them. All four were alive and healthy. They reported they had arrived on the island with only their clothes, two shovels, and 500 potatoes. Each had eaten one potato per day all year. How did they get enough potatoes?

Each person could have eaten one potato per day for 100 days, using 400 potatoes. The remaining 100 potatoes could have been planted, yielding as many as 2,000 potatoes (100 potatoes × 4 plants each × 5 potatoes average per plant).

think the potato had its beginnings around Lake Titicaca, where the tubers grew wild.

More than 7,000 years ago, the people who roamed through the Andes Mountains collected potatoes. Over hundreds of years they developed methods for growing them.

The Incas and the Potato

About 900 years ago, a small group of people, the Incas, settled in the Andes Mountains around Lake Titicaca. Like the Andean Indians before them, the Incas cultivated potatoes, corn, and beans.

Using knowledge from their ancestors, the Incas turned steep mountainsides into farmland. They leveled small areas of the mountainsides into *terraces*, flattened land areas. They also constructed canals to carry water for irrigating their crops from one field to another.

Their farming methods allowed the Incas to grow many different kinds of potatoes as well as corn and beans. Growing a variety of crops helped ensure against food shortages. If one crop failed, another was likely to survive and provide enough food for everyone. The potato was the Incas' most important crop and helped the civilization grow into a huge empire. Knowledge of the potato and the Incas' farming methods had spread to people in other areas of South America by 1492.

The Incas clearly understood the importance of the lowly potato to their empire. In their art forms, they used images of the potato. They even worshiped potato spirits in religious ceremonies.

To preserve their potatoes, the Incas made them into *chuño*, a dried potato product that can be stored for several years. To make chuño, they spread potatoes on the ground and left them overnight to freeze. The next day the Incas walked on the potatoes to squeeze the water out of them, then left them to dry in the sun. This process was repeated for four or five days until the potatoes were thoroughly dry. Today, descendants of the Incas still make and eat chuño.

The Potato Spreads to Europe

When the Spanish conquistadors arrived in South America in 1531, they were mostly interested in the Incas' gold and

Potato Pottery
The Incas did not leave a written history, but they did leave some evidence, in the form of pottery, of how they lived and what they valued.

The pot above was dug up by scientists in the Inca homeland of Peru. Notice how the artist who created this pot used images of potato "eyes" as decoration. This pot and others similar to it helped anthropologists understand that the Incas considered the potato very important.

Think of something important in your daily life that you could represent in a piece of pottery. Using clay, create a dish or pot with that image as decoration.

Armengol and his family live in the Andes Mountains in Peru. Like the ancient Incas, they grow potatoes and make chuño.

silver. To mine the precious metals, the conquistadors made slaves of the Incas and fed them chuño from the Inca storehouses throughout their empire.

We do not know exactly when and how the potato traveled from Peru to Europe and North America. We do know that the Spanish conquistadors fed potatoes to the sailors on their ships. Historians think the potato was taken by Spanish sailors from South American ports to Europe, especially Spain.

The potato was not an immediate hit in Europe. Because the potato was not mentioned in the Bible, many people believed humans should not eat it. Agriculture experts in France thought potato plants would destroy the soil. Some medical experts of the time thought the potato would cause disease in humans.

Despite these beliefs, farmers in northern Spain began to grow potatoes around 1600. From this European beginning, the potato's growth and use spread throughout Europe in the 1600s and 1700s.

The potato became a staple food of Europe for some of the same reasons it had been a basic food of the Andean peoples. Potatoes were easy to grow, and they grew in many

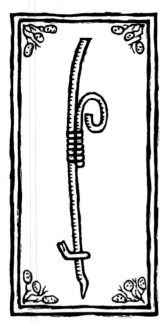

Incan digging tool for planting potatoes.

PLANTING POTATOES

The drawing on the right shows ancient Inca farmers using a digging tool to make holes in which to plant potato pieces. On the opposite page is an 1880s painting by the famous artist Vincent van Gogh. Look at the tool being used by the farmers in the painting. How is it like the digging tool of the Incas? Why do you think the Europeans adopted the Incas' farming tool as well as their potato plants?

As potatoes became a popular food in other cultures, tools for preparing potatoes were shared. What tools do you use at home to prepare potatoes?

Detail from a European painting titled Planting Potatoes.

climates and soils. In addition, they provided much of the nutrition people needed. By the middle of the 1800s, the potato had become one of Europe's most important foods.

The Potato Changes Europe

Before the first potato was brought to Europe by travelers from the Americas, almost all people in Europe were farmers. They grew grains such as wheat and rye and vegetables such as cabbages and beets. Most farmers could grow only the amount of food they needed to survive.

As European farmers obtained and learned more about potatoes, they began to plant them. They soon discovered that potato plants were easy to grow and produced many potatoes—more than one family could eat. The farmers sold the potatoes they did not need.

With fewer farmers needed to produce a steady supply of food, many farm workers moved to cities. They worked in factories and ran machines to make cloth, clothing, tools, and other products. With the money they earned in factories, the workers bought from farmers the food they needed—including potatoes. These workers were involved in the industrialization of Europe. *Industrialization* is the process of using machines to do work previously done by people.

Industrialization changed Europe from a continent of small farms and villages to a continent of manufacturing

The Potato in North America

The potato was brought to North America in 1719. As in Europe, it was not a success in North America for many years. In fact, potatoes did not become popular until the third U.S. president, Thomas Jefferson, served them at a White House dinner.

How does a food become popular today? Can you think of a food that has become popular in your lifetime? Pretend you have just discovered a new food and want to encourage people to start eating it. Create a television commercial for the food to help it catch on with the public.

cities. Without a reliable supply of inexpensive, nutritious potatoes, industrialization of Europe would have been more difficult and much slower.

Ireland: When the Potato Failed

Nowhere in Europe did the potato become more important than in the small island country of Ireland, west of England. For years the Irish had trouble growing enough food, especially in western Ireland. Poor soil, combined with too much or too little rain, made farming a difficult business.

In the mid-1600s the potato was brought to Ireland by Spanish fishermen. Eager for a reliable crop, the Irish soon learned how to grow potato plants. Potatoes grew well in the rocky soil of Ireland. A potato crop required less time and effort by farmers than their other crops, such as rye and barley. They discovered that the number of potatoes produced on just one acre of land could feed a family for a year.

POTATOES, WAR, AND TAXES

Before and after 1492, Europe was the scene of many wars. Soldiers fed themselves by raiding the storehouses of farmers. Unlike other crops, potatoes did not have to be stored. Farmers could leave them in the ground until they needed them. Because armies did not want to take time to dig up their next meal, the farmers' potato crops were usually spared.

Potatoes also saved farmers from tax collectors. In those days, farmers paid taxes to officials in the form of crops rather than money. Tax collectors could easily see and count the amount of grain stored in a warehouse, but they could not count the potatoes in the ground. So potatoes often were left untaxed.

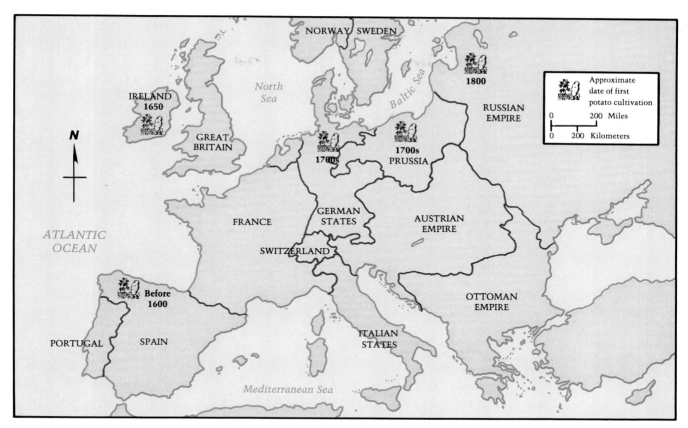

The Spread of the Potato in Europe. *Each date indicates the approximate year in which potatoes were first grown in the country indicated.*

One historian describes the importance of the potato to Irish farmers this way.

> *A strip [of land] between 500 and 800 yards long would provide enough potatoes for one family. Supplemented with milk, pork, bacon, cheese, or the blood of a cow, they would provide a balanced diet.*

Over time, Ireland's farmers stopped growing almost all other crops and planted mostly potatoes. The Irish population thrived on the vegetable. In 1760, Ireland had one and a half million people. By 1840, only eighty years later, it had nine million people—all potato eaters.

Then disaster struck Ireland. In June 1845, a potato blight began, and it continued for two years. A *blight* is a disease that kills plants. In only a few weeks, Ireland's potato crop was dead. The following description tells how fast the blight spread:

A blighted potato plant.

Immigrants arriving in New York City. The ships they traveled on were crowded, and often food was in short supply.

Starving Irish children digging for potatoes.

In 1845 a man passed through a certain district on his way to Cork for a week's stay with some relatives. On his way south all looked well. On his way back, however, the whole parish was strickened as if by frost, and the fields were black with devastated foliage.

Farmers had planted few other crops. Even the potatoes they left in the ground for storage were ruined by the blight. Without products to sell, farmers were forced off the land they farmed and had no other way to make a living. Hundreds of thousands died of starvation.

To escape death, thousands of Irish came to America by ship. Once in America, many of the Irish immigrants made their homes in east coast cities, especially New York and Boston. Irish men often took jobs building railroads and digging canals. Many Irish women worked in sewing rooms.

AN IMMIGRANT'S LETTER

The migration from Ireland and other European countries continued for years. Many immigrants were young, still in their teens. One young man named Patrick Murphy came to New York City from Ireland. He described his life in a letter to his mother.

An Irish immigrant.

September 15, 1885

My dear Mother,

I hope that you are very well, as I am. This letter is written for me by Tom Rooney, for I am no scholar. You remember how much more time I spent in the hills than in the schoolroom. As I told you in my last, I am stopping with Tom and his wife, Sally, who are fine people, so you should not worry about me. I am very comfortable and eat well.

Now that I am here a while, I like it better than ever. New York is a grand handsome city. But you would hardly know you had left Ireland, there are so many Irish people here. Some of them are become rich. Some of them are big men in government. For most of us it is hard work, but there is plenty of it and the pay is all right. They are always building things here. Tom worked on the great bridge they made over the river to Brooklyn a year or two ago. Now he has got me a job working with him on the new streets they are making in this city. There is always something going on if a man wants work.

Soon I will be sending you some money I have saved. I know that will help you and you will not feel so bad about how I had to leave you. Well, Mother, I must end now. I hope God has you in his keeping and gives you good health. There are plenty of good Catholic people here, and no fear of losing our way, as Father Dwyer said. Give my dearest love to John, Mary and Nora, and greetings to all my friends. I will write again soon.

Your son,

Pat

The Potato Today and Tomorrow

The next time you eat a potato, think about its long journey from the Andes Mountains to your plate. Consider that more than 7,000 years ago people ate potatoes much like the potatoes you eat today. Recall the advanced farming methods the Incas developed to grow potatoes as a reliable crop. Remember that in fewer than 100 years, potatoes helped Europe industrialize. Think about the millions of immigrants from Europe who came to the United States when their potato crops failed.

Don't be tempted to think the story of the potato's journey ends with massive European emigration to the United States. In the 100 years since that emigration, the potato has continued to find its way into the agriculture and diet of 130 of the world's 170 countries. For example, China today harvests more than twice as many potatoes as all the countries from Panama north through Canada.

MANY KINDS OF POTATOES

You probably didn't know that there are thousands of different varieties of potatoes. Potatoes come in many shapes and in colors ranging from rainbow pastels to bright reds and deep purples.

Four basic kinds of potatoes are shown here. All four can be prepared in many ways. The russet, a long brown potato, is generally considered the best for baking. The smaller red and white round potatoes are

russet

red

small white

long white

good for boiling. The long white is best for making potato chips.

In the United States, farmers do not grow all the varieties of potatoes that are produced in other parts of the world. However, the four basic kinds of potatoes are available in most states.

The next time you are in a grocery store, visit the produce section. How many colors and sizes of potatoes can you find? How many kinds do you eat?

A field of flowering potato plants. Each American eats an average of 126 pounds of potatoes per year!

Is the story of how the potato spread now over? Many experts think not. Scientists are developing potato seeds that can be planted instead of potato pieces. Seeds will make planting easier and increase potato production.

Scientists are also looking at the potato for help in feeding some of the world's people who face constant starvation. They point out that the potato grows quickly, can be adapted to harsh or mild climates, and provides more nutrition on less land than many other crops. The potato may indeed become a lifesaver in some regions of Africa and Asia where it is not now grown.

In the future, the potato's value may not be limited to feeding people. Someday we may also put potatoes in our cars' gas tanks—after the potatoes have been made into fuel.

The Power of the Potato

Is the potato really powerful? Five hundred years ago, Columbus and the later Spanish conquistadors came to the Americas in search of gold and silver to make them rich. They were not much interested in the potatoes they saw being grown by the Incas and others. Perhaps they should have paid more attention to the potato. Today, one year's worldwide potato crop is worth more money than all the gold the Spanish ever took from the Americas.

Ancient Farmers Teach Modern Farmers
Near Lake Titicaca in Bolivia, modern scientists discovered a 3,000-year-old system of canals and raised fields. After restoring the ancient system, farmers were amazed to find that the pre-Incan and Incan old ways produced seven times more potatoes than their new ways.

Can you think of other old ways that might be better than new ways? How about recycling and conserving our natural resources? Ask an adult at home to help you compare old and new technologies and old and new ways of living.

6

THE LEGENDARY HORSE
Enemy, Partner, Friend

*Do you know, gentlemen, it appears to me that
these Indians have great fear of our horses.*

Hernán Cortés made this observation in 1519 when he and
his horse-mounted conquistadors (conquerors) began their
march through the Aztec empire. The statement was recorded by Bernal Díaz del Castillo, Spanish writer and historian,
who served in Cortés's army. When some of the Aztecs first
saw a mounted conquistador, wrote Díaz, they thought the
man and horse were one beast. If this claim is true, the
Aztecs' false impression did not last long.

In only months, the Aztecs learned that the horse was
the constant companion of the conquistador. They realized
the great advantage horses gave Spanish soldiers over Aztec
warriors. Along with disease, the horse would become the
Aztecs' greatest enemy as they attempted to save their empire from the Spanish conquerors.

Why was the horse an unknown animal to the Aztecs
and other native peoples in the Americas? The story begins
thousands of years before Cortés's march.

Taming the Horse

Anthropologists believe that more than 10,000 years ago,
wild horses lived in the grasslands of Europe, Asia, and the
Americas. Near the end of the Ice Ages, horses became
extinct in the Americas, but they lived on in Europe and
Asia. Ancient people living near the Volga River in the area
where Europe and Asia join are thought to have been the
first humans to domesticate the horse. *Domesticate* means
to raise and train for human use.

The horse's domestication 6,000 years ago was a
significant development in human history because the horse
provided speed and power to help carry, plow, hunt, and
fight enemies. Having a treasure too good to keep in eastern
Europe, migrants, in time, took domesticated horses with
them to China and Mongolia in Asia and to areas around the
Mediterranean Sea.

*Opposite page: Lone
horse in the Navajo
Tribal Park, Arizona.*

Horse or Dog?
**Many experts accept the
theory that the word *horse*
comes from an ancient term
meaning "swift" or "run-
ning." Upon seeing horses
for the first time, some
Indians encountered by the
conquistadors called the
animals "sky dogs." They
believed the horses were
monsters or messengers of
the gods. Later, members of
Canada's Piegan tribe called
the horse *ponokomita*, "elk
dog," because it was the
size of an elk and carried
things like a dog.**

Thousands of years later, along the Mediterranean coast of northern Africa, Moslem people, called Moors, became especially good horse breeders and riders. When they crossed the Mediterranean into southern Europe to invade Spain, they took their fast and well-trained horses. The horses gave them the advantage they needed to defeat the Spanish.

The victory convinced the Spanish of the Moors' superior horses and riding ability. Over the next several hundred years, the Spanish learned to raise and ride this kind of horse. By 1492, the Spanish were Europe's finest horse riders. Having fought wars with mounted soldiers, they knew the value of horses in military conflict.

Horses in the Americas

The horse returned to the Americas on Columbus's second voyage in 1493. After being extinct in the Americas for 10,000 years, horses thrived on the lush vegetation and lack

SOUTH AMERICAN *GAUCHOS*

Before the Spanish arrived in South America, Indians hunted on the pampas, or plains, of present-day Argentina, Uruguay, Paraguay, and Brazil. On foot, they chased camel-like guanacos and other wild game and captured them with *bolas*, long ropes with heavy rocks tied to each end. A hunter swung a bola over his head until it was spinning, then released it in full swing. Striking the animal, the bola wrapped around its legs and prevented it from running away.

After the Spanish arrived in South America, the pampas hunters began to use both horses and the Spanish *lazo*, or lasso, along with bolas in their hunting. These roaming cowboys, often of mixed Spanish and Indian ancestry, became known as *gauchos*.

Compare the South American gauchos with images you have seen of cowboys in the American West. How do you think their lives were alike and different?

Spanish conquistadors were excellent riders and knew the value of their horses. They often said, "After God, we owe the victory to the horses."

of disease in the Caribbean. Later explorers who brought horses on their ships to leave on the islands were pleased when they returned to see that the wild herds had multiplied.

The voyage across the Atlantic Ocean was not easy for horses. Within two bands thirty degrees north and thirty degrees south of the equator, ships often stopped sailing because there was no wind. Horses on board died from the heat and the lack of water and had to be thrown overboard. These locations in the Atlantic earned the name *horse latitudes*.

As the Caribbean islands became the launching bases for explorations onto the South and North American continents, European settlers in the islands began raising horses for the explorers. This practice eliminated the need for the explorers to bring horses from Europe and assured them of good, healthy horses to take with them onto the mainlands. Cortés and his army invaded Mexico riding horses bred in Cuba. One Spanish historian who traveled with Cortés to the Caribbean wrote,

> *The horses multiplied in the Indies [the Caribbean] and became most excellent, in some places being even as good as the best in Spain, good not only for fast messenger work, but also for war and parade.*

The Spanish created clever ways to load horses onto ships.

This sixteenth-century illustration shows the advantage horses gave the conquistadors over the Aztecs.

The Horse and North American Indians

In battling Cortés's conquistadors, the Aztecs were only the first of the mainland Indians to experience the disadvantage of enemies on horseback. Cortés and later European explorers traveled the Americas on horses—often looting and killing Indians along the way. Indians quickly realized the value of owning horses.

Recognizing that the horse was one of their most powerful weapons, the Spanish tried to keep Indians from getting their horses. However, Indians were able to capture some runaway horses and steal others. Some they got from *commancheros*, people of mixed Spanish and Indian heritage who traded the horses for Indian goods. Some Indians were taught to be cowboys, called *vaqueros* in Spanish, by Spanish missionaries. Working in the missions, often as slaves, Indians learned to breed as well as ride horses. Still, the number of Indians owning horses was small.

In 1680, an event occurred that would change the lives of most Indians throughout the West and Great Plains of what is now the United States. Near Santa Fe, New Mexico, Pueblo Indians, who had been treated badly by the Spanish, rose up against the foreigners. In this war, known as the Pueblo Revolt, the Indians massacred or drove out the Spanish settlers and captured or set free thousands of their horses. The freed horses probably began the first herds of mustang and other wild horses in the West.

Using the horses they captured after the Pueblo Revolt, Indians could hunt buffalo more efficiently on horseback than on foot. Plains Indians could more easily move their people and belongings from camp to camp in search of better food supplies. Equally important, Indians could use horses to make war on their enemies—both other Indians and Europeans. For tribes that acquired guns from Europeans at about the same time they got horses, warfare became more frequent and more violent. Within 100 years after the Pueblo Revolt, the horse, along with the gun, had

HISPANIC HERITAGE

It's nearly impossible to imagine American cowboys without saddles and ropes, but their knowledge of this equipment came from Spain. In fact, American cowboys have made only slight changes in the saddles brought to the Americas from Spain. The American cowboy adapted the roping techniques of the vaqueros, who learned to rope from Spanish missionaries.

The word *Hispanic* is used to describe people and things having a common beginning in Spain. Hispanic comes from the Spanish word *Hispania*, an old name for Spain. We can hear the Hispanic heritage in the language of the American cowboy. The Spanish word *chaparejos* became the American word "chaps." *La reata* became "lariat," a cowboy rope. Even the term *vaquero* was turned into the American "buckaroo."

Can you point out the chaparejos and reata of the vaquero pictured here?

dramatically changed the lives of Plains Indians. *Plains Indians* lived in the plains areas of central North America.

The Horse of Myth and Legend

As a treasured possession of many Indian tribes, the horse became the subject of much Indian art and legend. Horse images were woven into blankets and baskets and painted on hides and rock walls by Plains and western Indians. The horse also appeared often in their myths and legends, handed down from generation to generation.

The Indian legend that follows is from the book *The Ways of My Grandmothers* by Beverly Hungry Wolf. She is a member of the Blood Indian tribe, a division of the Blackfoot Nation, which is located in southwestern Canada and northwestern Montana.

REUNITING THE NEZ PERCÉ AND THE APPALOOSA

The Appaloosa is a spotted horse that was bred by the Nez Percé Indians in present-day Washington state. In 1877, the U.S. government sent the Nez Percé to a reservation in Oklahoma—without their horses. Later, the tribe returned to live in northern Idaho, near their former homeland.

In early 1991 an Appaloosa horse breeder, Bob Browning of Farmington, New Mexico, gave fifteen Appaloosa horses to the Nez Percé. Browning's purpose was to reunite the tribe with the Appaloosa. The gift may be a rebirth for the tribe. As one tribal member said, "We can't get back our land or our horses, but we can get back our dignity. A lot of things have happened in our history, and it would be nice to feel good about ourselves again."

Alan Pinkerton, Sr., former Nez Percé tribal chairman, with one of his tribe's Appaloosas.

The horse gave the Plains Indian power over the buffalo. John Inness's painting **The Buffalo Hunt** *shows the Indians' skill with horses.*

In reading this myth, think about how the story uses the image of a horse as a symbol of a loved one who has left the tribe.

The Horse Woman

Long ago a camp of Blood people was moving from one place to another. As they went along a pack load belonging to a young woman came loose and fell to the ground. She stopped to repack while the rest of the people went on toward their new campground. Not long after they were gone, a handsome young man stepped out from the bushes and stood in front of the woman. She became quite frightened and told him to leave her alone, as she already had a husband. But the man forced her to go with him. That evening the woman's husband came back to look for her, but all he found was the partly tied pack laying where she left it. He figured that she had been captured by an enemy, and he mourned her loss.

Some years later it so happened that the same group of people again camped by this place. While they were there they discovered a herd of wild horses, and someone noticed that there seemed to be a person among them. The warriors quickly went after the herd and were able to rope the strange person. It had the

Beverly Hungry Wolf

head and chest of a woman, but the body and legs of a horse, all covered with hair. She fought and reared just like a wild horse, and a colt whinnied to her when the warriors finally dragged her away.

Back at the camp the woman's husband recognized her, but she would have nothing to do with him, or with anyone else. She struggled to get free just like a wild animal. Finally the husband said that there was no use in keeping her tied up, so they let her go and watched her race away after the horse herd. No one ever saw her again.

Cattle, Cowboys, and the Horse

When most people watch cowboys rounding up cattle in a movie, they think of the American West. However, ranching was a Spanish idea. Along with the horses the Spanish brought from Spain, they brought cattle and cattle ranching skills. The Spanish established their first cattle ranches in Mexico on Aztec lands. Other Spanish settlers began ranches in present-day California, Arizona, New Mexico,

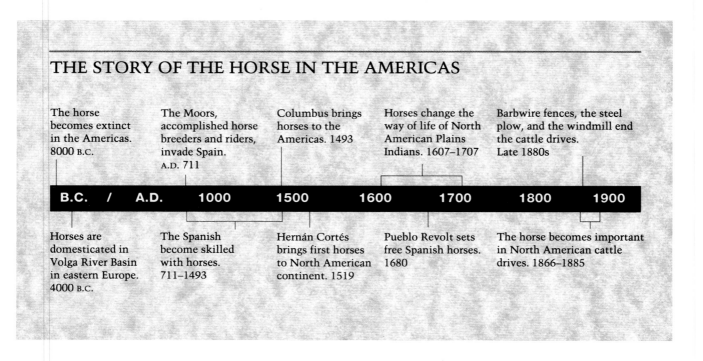

THE STORY OF THE HORSE IN THE AMERICAS

The horse becomes extinct in the Americas. 8000 B.C.

The Moors, accomplished horse breeders and riders, invade Spain. A.D. 711

Columbus brings horses to the Americas. 1493

Horses change the way of life of North American Plains Indians. 1607–1707

Barbwire fences, the steel plow, and the windmill end the cattle drives. Late 1880s

B.C. / A.D. 1000 1500 1600 1700 1800 1900

Horses are domesticated in Volga River Basin in eastern Europe. 4000 B.C.

The Spanish become skilled with horses. 711–1493

Hernán Cortés brings first horses to North American continent. 1519

Pueblo Revolt sets free Spanish horses. 1680

The horse becomes important in North American cattle drives. 1866–1885

and Texas. Everywhere they turned their cattle loose on the American grasslands, the herds multiplied and took over more and more Indian homelands.

After the Civil War ended in 1865, cattle ranching spread across the Great Plains into Oklahoma, Kansas, Nebraska, and Missouri. In the vast grasslands, cattle roamed unfenced until it was time to butcher them for beef.

RANCHING: A SPANISH INVENTION

Ranching and the activities associated with it—roundups, branding, and cattle drives—originated in Spain. For hundreds of years Spanish ranchers had been grazing herds of cattle, sheep, and other animals. The ranchers brought their experience with them to the Americas.

After Columbus brought the first herd of tough Iberian cattle to the Caribbean in 1493, cattle ranching quickly spread to Mexico, Brazil, and throughout South and then North America.

Spanish ranchers relied on their well-trained cow ponies to help manage the large herds of cattle. How might horses be useful in rounding up, driving, and branding cattle?

Among the cowboys on the cattle drives, about one in four was an African American. Rodeo star Bill Pickett was credited with creating bulldogging, or steer wrestling.

Railroads were built to get the cattle from the central and western regions of the United States to people along the east coast. Cattle towns such as Dodge City, Kansas, sprang up at the ends of the railroads. For about a 25-year period, cowboys on horseback rounded up and herded thousands of cattle across the hundreds of miles from Texas and New Mexico to the cattle towns. This was the golden age of the cowboys who became the heroes of western movies.

The cowboy era ended almost as quickly as it had begun. New farming inventions, including the steel plow and water pumps, allowed ranchers to plant, irrigate, and harvest corn for cattle feed. Barbwire fences kept cattle in smaller areas and eliminated the need for big round-ups. Railroads were extended farther into cattle country. In the heartland of North America, European cattle and Central American corn came together to create the world's largest livestock industry—and most cowboys found themselves out of work.

COWBOY SKILLS

Although the number of ranch cowboys declined after about 1900, the sport of rodeo provided new opportunities for cowboys to display their skills. For example, their skill at taming wild horses led to the broncobusting rodeo event (see the photograph). Training horses to run fast, stop suddenly, and make quick turns led to events such as races and trick riding.

Think about some of the ranching jobs cowboys performed with horses—roping, herding, and riding wild horses until they were tamed. Write descriptions of rodeo sporting events that could be created from cowboys' regular ranch work.

Many people enjoy the thrill of horse jumping and other riding sports.

The Horse Today

For nearly 6,000 years after its domestication, the horse played a critical role in human life. Horses carried heavy loads, plowed fields, and went to battle with their masters. They were roped, harnessed, ridden, spurred, raced, and bred. Almost without exception, the horse's human partners respected and valued these animals, often admiring them in art and literature.

About 100 years ago, the role of the horse in the Americas began to change. New methods of transportation reduced the horse's value. Modern engines replaced original horsepower with machine power. Even the horse's ranch jobs were taken over by four-wheel-drive vehicles and occasionally helicopters. Despite its changing role, the horse continued to be admired and respected by humans.

Today, the horse is used mostly for sports and recreation. Some horse owners take great pride in working with or watching their horses compete in races, shows, and rodeos. Others enjoy their horses as family pets. Whatever its role in the future, the horse—a native returned to the Americas after 10,000 years of absence—has left an unforgettable mark on the history of the American continents.

What Is Horsepower? Perhaps you have heard someone talk about an automobile's horsepower. Horsepower measures the power of motors and engines. The term was created by Scottish engineer James Watt about 200 years ago to compare the power of a steam engine to the power of heavy work horses. A one-horsepower engine has the power of one- and one-half draft (work) horses. A 100-horse power automobile engine represents the power of how many draft horses?

Answer: 150.

7 BITTERSWEET SUGAR
The Root of Slavery

Opposite page: African slaves cutting sugarcane on a plantation.

Do you like sweet food and drinks? Most people do. Sugar is used as an ingredient in many foods, such as candy and soft drinks. Many people add sugar to cereal, coffee, and other foods to make them taste sweeter. Some experts say humans have a built-in liking for sweet tastes. It is no surprise, then, that sugar is popular around the world.

What Is Sugar?

The sugar you see in sugar bowls and find in many foods is called sucrose, which comes from the juice in sugar beets and sugarcane. Sugar from beets has been produced in large amounts for only about 150 years. Sugar from cane has been produced much longer—about 10,000 years.

Sugar is not necessary for the human diet. In fact, eating too much sugar can cause people to gain weight, suffer tooth decay, and be more likely to develop certain diseases. Some experts believe that after narcotic drugs, alcohol, and tobacco, sugar is the most harmful substance craved by humans.

Growing Sugarcane

Sugarcane is a grass whose stalks contain a juice from which sucrose is made. Mature cane stalks are about two inches thick and twelve to fifteen feet high. Eight to twelve months after planting, they are ready for cutting.

Sugarcane must be cut as soon as it ripens. The stalks are tough and difficult to cut through, even with today's machines. Hundreds of years ago, people cut sugarcane with a large steel knife. The knife blade was about five inches wide and eighteen inches long. After cutting, the stalks were piled into carts and hurried to the mill, where they were ground up as quickly as possible in order to extract the juice. The rapid pace was very tiring and dangerous for both the animals and the humans who ran the mill machinery.

To produce sugar crystals, the extracted juice had to be boiled immediately. Sugar boilers were highly skilled, but the heat, noise, fast pace, and danger made their work extremely difficult.

You and Sugar
Experts estimate that each person in the United States uses about 100 pounds of sugar each year—nearly 2 pounds of sugar each week! For one week, keep track of the amount of pure sugar and the foods containing sucrose that you eat. Do you use more or less sugar than the national average?

A mill for extracting juice from sugarcane by grinding the stalks. This mill with three vertical rollers was the most efficient one available in the early 1600s.

The sugarcane industry in the Americas began in the Caribbean almost 500 years ago, just a few years after Columbus landed in the islands. Sugarcane grew well in the islands but required large numbers of workers to plant, harvest, and process it into sugar.

Sugar Demand in Europe

The need for sugarcane workers in the Caribbean was driven by the demand for sugar in Europe. Before about A.D. 1000, people in northern Europe had not yet tasted sugar. Moors traveling from North Africa to Spain had brought sugarcane with them around 900. The use of sugar, produced in Spain and Portugal, gradually spread north. By about 1600, English royalty and rich people, the first people in England to learn about sugar, demanded a steady supply.

Over a 200-year period, use of sugar spread from the upper classes to the common people. It became a popular ingredient in the diet of English people and other Europeans. Although sugar may have first been used as a medicine or spice, its popularity grew as a sweetener for tea, coffee, and chocolate. Later, it became a common cooking ingredient. By 1800 Europeans, especially the English, wanted sugar—lots of it—and they paid high prices for it.

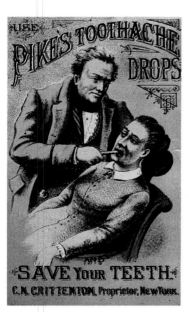

Since its introduction into our diets, sugar has contributed to toothaches and tooth decay.

Sugar in the Americas

Columbus brought sugarcane to the Americas on his second voyage in 1493. It grew so well that in a few years there was enough sugarcane to ship some to Europe. The first sugarcane to reach Europe from the Caribbean was shipped from the island of Hispaniola in 1516.

The European planters who began the sugarcane industry in the Caribbean thought the Indians living on the islands could be enslaved to provide the labor needed. However, many Indians died from the contagious diseases brought to the islands by the Europeans and from the brutal treatment by the foreigners. Some Indians refused to be enslaved and were killed or forced to flee. Lacking enough Indian workers or Europeans willing to work in sugarcane processing, the planters turned to Africa to supply the labor they needed.

A SLAVE'S DIARY

Olaudah Equiano was a slave on the island of Monserrat in the Caribbean. He was one of the fortunate slaves who received an education. When he was older, he wrote his life's story. In the entry below, Equiano describes his feeling when the slave ship he traveled on reached the Caribbean island where he was to be held captive.

At the sight of this land of bondage, a fresh horror ran through all my frame and chilled me to the heart. My former slavery [in Africa] now rose in dreadful review to my mind, and displayed nothing but misery, stripes, and chains. . . . I called upon God's thunder, and his avenging power, to direct the stroke of death to me, rather than permit me to become a slave, and be sold from lord to lord.

The horrors of slavery are almost more than we can imagine today. List all the things you would fear if you knew you had to be a slave for the rest of your life.

The planters knew that Africans previously had been enslaved by each other and by other Europeans.

With the demand for sugar growing by the year, Europeans claimed huge areas of land and turned them into plantations. *Plantations* are large farms on which crops are raised by many workers, often enslaved, who live on the farm. *Slavery*, the ownership of humans by other humans, was essential to the success of the plantation system. Without the labor of many, many slaves, plantation owners would not have made vast fortunes from producing sugar.

Plantations spread throughout the Caribbean islands and in some areas of Central and South America, especially present-day Brazil. Plantation owners came to the Caribbean from England, France, Portugal, and the Netherlands.

Slavery and the Middle Passage

Providing slaves to Caribbean plantation owners quickly became a business. Even before Columbus landed in the Americas, Europeans, especially the Portuguese, had set up a slave trade between Africa and Europe. Seeing this new

HOW MUCH ROOM?

In addition to being chained together, slaves were packed tightly between the decks of slave ships. Study the drawing of the slave ship. As the enlarged area shows, slaves were required to sit in a space three feet, three inches in height. This is a little more than the height of the space under a table.

With three or four classmates, crawl under a table and sit the way the slaves are sitting in the picture. How long could you comfortably sit in this position? How would you feel if you had sat in this position almost twenty-four hours a day for four to six weeks, as African slaves had to do?

Africans being forced to march to west African seaports, where they were sold to European slavers.

market, the slave traders, called *slavers*, turned their attention to developing a slave business in the Caribbean. The first African slaves probably reached the Caribbean in 1505.

Conflict among groups of people in Africa contributed to the European and American slave trades. Africans lived in many tribes and states. Clashes among them often led to wars, and victorious tribes held captive members of losing tribes. European and later American slavers sailed to Africa and bought these captives. Most Africans who became slaves were men, but there were women and children also.

Over nearly 400 years, at least ten million Africans were enslaved in the Americas. The majority came between 1700 and 1800 when European demand for sugar was highest. The Africans worked on Spanish, English, Dutch, and French plantations throughout the Caribbean. Their labor also supported the Portuguese plantations of Brazil and other European plantations in Mexico and South America. In the 1700s, enslaved Africans were taken to the Spanish territories and English colonies in the United States.

The African slave trade had three parts, or passages. First, the captives were forced to march to west African seaports, where they were sold. Once sold, they were branded with a red-hot branding iron to show they were slaves and to identify their owners. They were chained together, two by two, and packed between the decks of slave ships.

The slave ship voyage from western Africa to the Caribbean sugar plantations was the second part of the journey—the *Middle Passage*. The 4,000-mile trip, which took many weeks, was a nightmare come to life. Some slaves preferred death to slavery and committed suicide by jumping overboard. Many died from eating spoiled food and getting diseases. Historians have estimated that as many as one in three slaves died in the Middle Passage. The third part of the trip occurred when the slaves were sold in the Caribbean and sent to plantations in the islands and in Brazil.

Triangle Trade

By 1700, the Europeans' desire for sugar was just one of several trade demands by people living on the continents around the Atlantic Ocean. People in the American colonies wanted molasses, another sugarcane product, for making rum. People in Africa wanted American rum. Plantation owners in the Americas wanted more slaves. These demands led to regular patterns of trade among people in the Americas, Europe, and Africa. The routes of trade ships created giant triangles across the Atlantic Ocean.

Here's how one triangle trade pattern worked. Trade ship captains bought molasses from ports in the Caribbean

A slave ship.

SLAVE TRADE AND PROFIT

Captain Theophilus Conneau was a slaver in the early 1800s. In 1827, he was part-owner of the slave ship *Fortuna*. At the right are his income and expenses record for a four-month slave voyage.

Find the amount of Conneau's profit by subtracting expenses from the total income. **You are correct if you answer $41,719. In today's dollars, his profit would be about half a million dollars.**

With a friend discuss the question, "Does one human have the right to make money by selling other humans?"

Income	
Sale of cargo (217 slaves)	$77,469
Proceeds from vessel sold at auction	3,950
Total Income	**$81,419**
Expenses	
Vessel, fittings, cargo, wages	$39,700
Profit	**$**

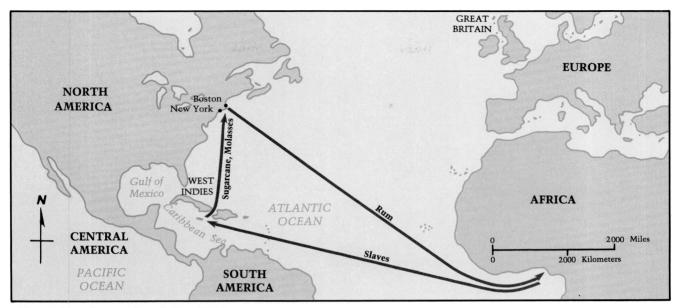

The Triangle Trade of the 1700s

and delivered their loads to cities such as Boston and New York in the English colonies. The molasses was sold to rum makers, who in turn sold rum they had already made to the ship captains. Sailing on to Africa, the ship captains sold their cargo of rum to Africans. From Africans, they bought slaves. The slaves were transported to the Caribbean and sold to plantation owners. Ship captains, merchants, and plantation owners made handsome profits in this trade.

Plantation Life for Slaves

Every Monday through Saturday, plantation slaves who worked in the fields and sugar processing plants began work before dawn. At about nine o'clock, slaves got a half-hour off to eat breakfast. They also had a break for a midday meal, sometimes an hour and a half. Meals, which often consisted of only boiled vegetables, were served in the fields. After the midday meal, the slaves worked until dark. Other slaves were craftsmen, animal tenders, and household servants, who also worked long hours.

Some plantation owners treated their slaves cruelly. Beatings were a common form of punishment. Members of slave families often were separated and never rejoined. Even the kindest owners took away their slaves' most important right—freedom.

Slaves generally were not required to work on Saturday afternoons or Sundays. Rather than rest from their grueling

Africans in the Caribbean developed markets in which they traded foods and crafts. The markets lasted long after slavery ended. This photograph, taken in about 1902, shows women on the way to a market in Jamaica, an island in the Caribbean.

work week, most slaves used this time to tend their own gardens, fix up their living quarters, and make crafts such as baskets and pottery. Many made a great effort to learn about the natural environment of the islands. They followed some of the farming and medical practices of the natives who first lived on the islands. When possible, they applied knowledge from their African heritage to their new environment. Unlike their European owners, the slaves discovered how to use native plants for food and medicine, where to find drinking water, and which clay to use for making pottery.

Perhaps the first contribution Africans made to the Americas of their own free will was their knowledge of ways to prepare tasty dishes from a wide variety of vegetables, fruits, meat, and fish. Drawing on African uses of spices and herbs to make foods taste better, the slaves experimented with the spices available in the Americas. The cooking skills of Africans forever changed the food tastes of people in the Americas, especially those in Brazil, the Caribbean, and the American South.

After Slavery

The Caribbean sugar industry went into slow decline after 1800. Wars and economic conditions in Europe lowered the

African-inspired Caribbean foods.

demand for sugar. At about the same time, farmers in Germany and France began to grow sugar beets. By the late 1800s, use of sugar from sugar beets had overtaken that from sugarcane. Slavery gradually was abolished in the Americas. In 1888, Brazil became the last country in the Americas to officially outlaw slavery.

Out of the sad history of sugar comes one highlight: the remarkable survival and adaptation of the enslaved Africans. Not only did thousands of these forced migrants manage to stay alive despite the brutality of their work, but they also adapted to their new environment with great skill. Unlike many of the plantation owners, the African slaves learned to use the natural resources and plants of the Caribbean and southern colonies to their advantage. They improved their own lives and shared their knowledge with other immigrants to the Americas.

Today, African contributions to food, art, music, writing, and community life enrich the lives of people throughout the Americas and the world.

Dr. Jessica B. Harris

AFRICAN FOODS

Dr. Jessica B. Harris, an expert on the African contribution to foods in the Americas, has written, "Black hands have turned wooden spoons in heavy cast-iron pots for centuries." Dr. Harris's statement gives rightful credit to African cooks in the Americas. For example, did you know that the recipe for peanut butter, the all-American food, was brought by Africans to the United States?

Here is Dr. Harris's recipe for peanut butter. You may want to write it on a recipe card and try making it at home with an adult's permission.

The recipe calls for roasted peanuts. Dr. Harris suggests roasting them as West Africans do by mixing unroasted peanuts in their shells with fresh, clean sand and then baking the mixture for thirty minutes in a 400-degree oven. Save the sand for another time, shell the peanuts, and enjoy.

Peanut Butter (West Africa)
Yield = 1½ cups
2 cups roasted peanuts
3 teaspoons peanut oil
salt to taste

Grind or coarsely chop the peanuts. Add the peanut oil and continue to mix until you have reached the desired crunchiness. Add salt to taste and stir to blend.

8 CHOICES FOR THE FUTURE
The Exchange Continues

The voyages of Columbus set off a 500-year period of exchanges between the two old worlds. Thousands of exchanges—plant, animal, human, technology, knowledge, disease—have occurred since 1492 and continue today. The speed of change continues to increase.

This book has focused on five "seeds," planted by the Columbus voyages, that led to great changes in both old worlds. These exchanges have had both beneficial and damaging consequences. Diseases, although an unplanned weapon, were a benefit to the Europeans in conquering the Indians of the Americas. For the Indians, smallpox and other diseases had only negative consequences. The horse also proved an unexpected ally of conquest by providing the Europeans speed and a means of transporting goods. Later, Indians acquired horses from the Europeans, and the animals proved beneficial to their lives.

The crop exchanges also had mixed consequences. In the 1500s, 1600s, and 1700s, the Indians' maize and

Opposite page: Earth from space.

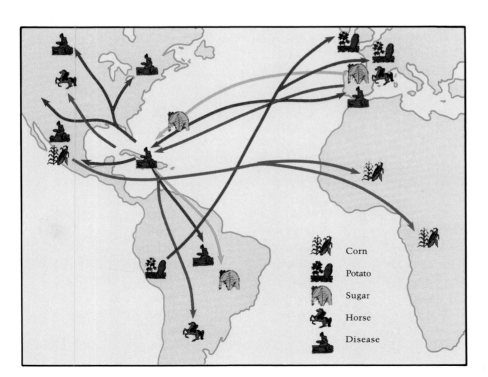

Corn

Potato

Sugar

Horse

Disease

Five Seeds of Change

potatoes saved millions of Europeans and Africans from starvation. On the other hand, corn played an unfortunate role in slavery when it was used to feed captive Africans on slave ships. The once life-saving potato forced millions of Europeans to leave their homelands when their potato crops failed in the 1800s. Although the successful production of sugarcane in the Americas fed the sweet tooth of Europe, it led to the enslavement of at least ten million Africans.

The story of how each seed was exchanged and what happened as a result of its exchange can be traced through historical writings, art, and objects left by our ancestors. As new evidence is collected and studied, we will continue to learn more about the ways these exchanges altered both the physical and the human worlds that existed in 1492.

The Human Exchange

Perhaps the most significant effect of the Europeans' encounter with the Americas was the human exchange. Beginning with Columbus's first voyage, the movement of

SPAGHETTI MEETS TOMATO

What happened when wheat flour from Europe met tomatoes from the Americas? Spaghetti with tomato sauce! This is only one of many new dishes created from food exchanges between the two old worlds. Name other dishes made from combinations of the foods listed here.

Foods from the Americas	Foods from Europe, Asia, and Africa
Avocados	Bananas
Beans	Barley
Chile peppers	Beets
Cocoa	Cabbage
Corn	Cattle
Peanuts	Grapes
Pineapples	Oats
Potatoes	Olives
Pumpkins	Onions
Squashes	Pigs
Sweet potatoes	Rice
Tomatoes	Sheep
Turkeys	Wheat

people among continents became the most massive in history. Although few American Indians crossed the oceans to settle on the other side of the world, millions of Europeans, Africans, and Asians made a one-way trip to the Americas.

Within fifteen years after Columbus's landing, the first of millions of Africans were being forced to come to the Americas. Decades later, large numbers of Europeans began to arrive. Between 1600 and 1800 more than ten million European immigrants came to North and South America. In the 1800s some fifty million Europeans landed in the Americas. Along with the Europeans, Asians and more Africans also came. After slavery ended, Africans emigrated to the Americas by choice rather than by force.

Immigrants to the Americas built new lives. They married and had families, often large families. Immigration and a high birth rate led to a population explosion. Today the current population of all the countries of North and South America exceeds 725 million! The United States alone has nearly 250 million people.

Immigrants added to the multicultural population of the Americas.

WORLD POPULATION GROWTH

Today, the world's population is thirteen times greater than it was in 1492. During the 80-year period between 1850 and 1930, the population doubled from 1 to 2 billion. During the 45 years between 1930 and 1975, the population doubled again to 4 billion. Some experts predict the world's population will be 6.3 billion by 2000 and may go over 10 billion by the year 2035. In Africa, the population doubles every 24 years and in Asia every 36 years. In the United States, it takes about 100 years for the population to double. Scientists are concerned that the earth cannot supply enough food to feed 10 billion people.

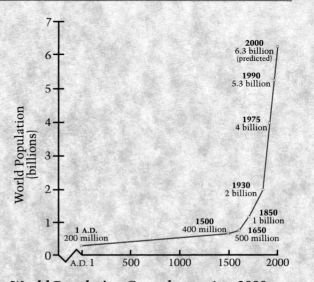

World Population Growth, A.D. 1 to 2000

Once the Americas were home only to the Indian descendants of the migrants who crossed the Bering land bridge. Today, the continents support a more diverse multicultural population. A *multicultural population* is one made up of people from different races and cultures. Our skin colors are of various hues and tones. We speak many languages and practice scores of religions. We do thousands of jobs and enjoy different kinds of music, art, and literature. We live in different countries and under different forms of government. Although conflicts sometimes arise from cultural intermixing, the merging of people's skills, ideas, and beliefs has created lively societies.

The Human Impact on Nature

The population explosion in the Americas has taken a great toll on the natural environment. No matter where people live, they have to be fed, clothed, and housed. To meet these needs, all 725 million people use natural resources—land, plants, animals, water, forests, minerals, and air.

The first Europeans to arrive in the Americas took back to Europe a vision of a land with seemingly endless

THE LIFE-SAVING OZONE LAYER

The ozone layer of the earth's atmosphere protects our planet from the sun's harmful ultraviolet rays. Chlorofluorocarbons (CFCs) are chemicals that contain chlorine, flourine, and carbon. When released into the air from air conditioning units, aerosol propellants, and cleaning fluids, CFCs destroy the ozone layer. With support from the United Nations, 93 countries have agreed to stop the production of CFCs by the end of the 1990s. Ask an adult at home to help you find newspaper reports on other ways nations are cooperating to save the environment.

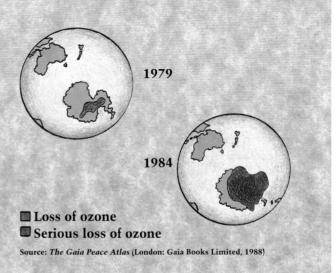

1979

1984

■ Loss of ozone
■ Serious loss of ozone

Source: *The Gaia Peace Atlas* (London: Gaia Books Limited, 1988)

Most garbage in the United States is buried in landfills, huge mounds of trash that eventually are covered with dirt. These landfills are filling up and closing at the rate of two per day.

resources. This vision led newcomers and their descendants to use up natural resources with little thought of consequences. Their guns destroyed wildlife. Forests fell to their axes and saws. Their plows and later their tractors buried the Great Plains' rich grasslands forever. The Americas' natural environment did not stand a chance against the dreams and actions of immigrants who flooded its shores.

Over the past 500 years, our air, land, and water have become polluted. Exhaust from automobiles, trucks, and factories creates brown clouds over our cities. Acid rain that forms in the clouds destroys lakes, forests, rivers, and crops. Americans' throwaway habits are leaving our land, waterways, and oceans unfit for living things. People, especially those in the United States, consume so many natural energy resources that some experts estimate the world has less than a 35-year known supply of oil and natural gas.

One environmental official has said, "For two hundred years we've been conquering nature. Now we're beating it to death." We can no longer escape to another "new world" on our planet to meet our demands. We can only limit our demands to match the earth's ability to supply them.

An Interdependent World

Today, the world's nations and people are parts of a global society. We are *interdependent,* which means that we rely on each other. Wherever people live in the world, they depend on one another for things they want and need. People in eastern Europe depend on wheat grown in Canada and

Oil is an important energy source, but it can cause environmental problems. Here, workers clean up an oil spill on a beach.

Many of the products we use affect wildlife. Do you recognize the plastic object around the gull's neck?

the United States. People in Europe and North America depend on oil from the Middle East. Modern transportation carries people and products where they are needed. Communication satellites keep the world's peoples in touch with each other day and night.

Interdependence makes all of us responsible for protecting our planet. Earth has only one atmosphere, and its oceans are all connected. Polluting the air in one part of the world or dumping poisons in one ocean can do harm around the globe. We all share nature's gifts. We also share responsibility for nature's destruction and pollution.

Choosing a Positive Future

Daily we hear and read about riots, civil war, terrorism, and other conflicts among people. These encounters threaten our world's survival. In the long run, worldwide environmental problems may be as threatening to our lives as human conflicts. To reduce this threat, we must become aware of our past mistakes and use our knowledge to stop the destruction of our earth.

Concerned people around the world are taking action to correct our environmental ills. Some have helped limit human use of parks and wilderness areas. Many have cleaned up lakes, rivers, and beaches. Others have helped pass laws to protect wildlife. More needs to be done.

We must start by realizing that *all* natural resources are limited. We can no longer waste resources or be greedy in our use of them. We can care for nature by leading simpler lives and demanding fewer products. We can use less electricity, walk instead of ride, and conserve water.

Author Diane MacEachern lists 750 everyday ways people can help clean up the earth in her book *Save Our Planet*. She introduces her book with these words:

> *Even though you are just one person who may never have done anything extraordinary before, you can change the world. It's true. Because everything you do— from the way you wash your clothes to how you heat your house to the kind of car you drive—either makes the world a better or worse place in which to live.*

One World

In 1492, two old but quite different worlds existed. When Columbus landed in the Caribbean, those two old worlds started to become more alike. The exchanges that happened as a result of that chance landing have created one world.

THE THREE Rs

Recycle, reuse, and reduce are actions people can take to improve our environment. To *recycle* is to create ways to use things in other forms. To *reuse* is to repair things instead of throwing them away. To *reduce* is to use less of something.

Conduct an inventory of your family's trash for one week. Divide a sheet of paper into three columns. In the columns, list items that could be recycled, reused, or reduced. Share your findings with your family and agree to take one action to reduce your family's use of natural resources.

Exchanges continue today. Although plants, animals, and diseases are still being exchanged, many present-day exchanges involve technology and information. Computers and satellite communication allow these exchanges and their consequences to happen quickly, often within months.

Five hundred years ago, people gave little thought to the environment. Today, we know that the planet's natural resources cannot last forever at the rates we are using them. Scientist Carl Sagan has written,

> We stand today at a great branch point in human history. During the million years or so that humans have inhabited the Earth, there have been many points at which our ancestors turned toward one of many possible futures: What we in this century must decide is whether we will have a future at all.

By working together as individuals and as groups, we can save our planet and ourselves. As we plant the seeds of change for our future, we must do so with concern for all people and for the environment we all share. The challenge is global, but the choices belong to each of us.

SILENT SPRING

Imagine a spring without the sound of birds singing. In 1962 Rachel Carson's book, *Silent Spring*, warned readers that such a spring was possible if the use of *pesticides*, chemicals to kill unwanted pests, were not controlled. As a sea-life biologist, Carson had studied the interdependence of all living things. Through her research, she identified examples of how pesticides not only were killing large numbers of birds and fish but also were poisoning the food supply of animals and humans. Carson's powerful writing, combined with her thorough research, raised the concern of citizens and led to laws restricting the use of pesticides.

ENVIRONMENTAL ACTION BULLETIN BOARD

Nature and Medicine

Many modern medicines have been developed from plants that grow in tropical rain forests. Researchers think they may be able to develop rain forest medicines to treat cancer and AIDS, two worldwide diseases.

Between 1945 and 1985, half the world's rain forests were destroyed to make way for farms and roads. In Brazil, a rain forest area the size of Nebraska is cut down each year. Destroyed along with the forests are the homes of rain forest Indians, rare wildlife, and the possibility of treatments for cancer and AIDS.

Recycling Action

- Some kinds of paper can be recycled seven or more times.
- Each American can save, on the average, six pounds of glass per month.
- United States cities and towns support more than 1,500 curbside recycling programs.
- A recent survey showed that 90 percent of Americans would support passing laws to force people to recycle.

What has your school or community done to promote recycling? What can you do to contribute?

A Survey

Ask ten people this question: "To reduce electricity use, would you be willing to turn off your television set for two hours between 6:00 P.M. and 10:00 P.M. each night?" Tally your results, then combine your results with those of your classmates. Write a report on your class findings for your school newspaper.

Environmental Facts

- Each year in the United States three million cars are abandoned.
- U.S. citizens recycle only 10 percent of their trash.
- Waxed paper is biodegradable but cannot be recycled.
- Thirty-five percent of the world's annual wood production goes into making paper products.
- Over 40 percent of our trash consists of paper.
- A family of four uses 100 gallons of water per day flushing the toilet.

As a class or with a group, collect additional facts about our environment. Put the facts into categories such as recycling, air pollution, trash, and so on, and create an environmental factbook.

GLOSSARY

anthropologist (ˌan(t)-thrə-ˈpäl-ə-jəst) Scientist who studies human beings, sometimes by examining objects left by earlier people, 5.

blight (ˈblīt) A disease affecting plants that causes them to stop growing or die, 53.

colony (ˈkäl-ə-nē) A group of people who settle in a new territory but retain ties with their parent state, 15.

conquistador (kȯŋ-ˈkēs-tə-ˌdȯ(ə)r) A Spanish conqueror of the Americas, 21.

domesticate (də-ˈmes-ti-ˌkāt) To train an animal or plant for use by human beings, 59.

epidemic (ˌep-ə-ˈdem-ik) An outbreak of an infectious disease that spreads rapidly among many people, 27.

ethanol (ˈeth-ə-ˌnȯl) Alcohol, made by fermenting corn, that can be used alone as a fuel or blended with gasoline, 45.

Hispania (his-ˈpān-ē-ə) An old, Latin name for Spain and Portugal, 63.

Hispanic (his-ˈpan-ik) Of or relating to people, speech, or culture with common beginnings in Spain and Portugal, 63.

horse latitudes (ˈhȯ(ə)rs ˈlat-ə-ˌt(y)üds) Either of two regions near 30° N or 30° S latitudes, characterized by high pressure calms and light, unpredictable winds, 61.

immunity (im-ˈyü-nət-ē) A condition of being able to resist a particular disease, 27.

Indies (ˈin-(ˌ)dēz) A term used by Columbus and other Europeans to describe the present-day countries of China, Japan, Indonesia, and India, 7.

industrialization (in-ˌdəs-trē-ə-lə-ˈzā-shən) The process of converting to the use of machines to do work previously done by people, 51.

infectious disease (in-ˈfek-shəs diz-ˈēz) A condition of poor health resulting from the introduction of certain microorganisms into the body; spread from person to person, sometimes through the air, 27.

interdependent (in-ˌtər-di-ˈpen-dənt) Relying upon each other for help or support, 85.

Kachina (kə-ˈchē-nə) A spirit worshiped by Hopi Indians, often represented in the form of a doll, 43.

maize (ˈmāz) Indian corn, 37.

middle passage (ˈmid-ˈl ˈpas-ij) In slave trade, the second portion of the slaves' journey during which they were transported by ship from Africa to the Caribbean islands, 76.

multicultural population (ˌməl-tē-ˈkəlch(-ə)-rəl ˌpäp-yə-ˈlā-shən) People of a country or region who have more than one racial or ethnic background, 84.

nomadic (nō-ˈmad-ik) Of or relating to a group of people who rove from place to place, 19.

pesticide (ˈpes-tə-ˌsīd) An agent, often a chemical, used to kill unwanted pests, 88.

plantation (plan-ˈtā-shən) A large farm, usually worked by enslaved laborers, 74.

recycle ((ˈ)rē-ˈsī-kəl) To use something over again or in different forms, 87.

reduce (ri-ˈd(y)üs) To use less in amount or number of something, 87.

reuse ((ˈ)rē-ˈyüz) To repair objects rather than throw them away, 87.

slaver (ˈslā-vər) A person who takes part in slave trade, 75.

slavery (ˈslāv-(ə-)rē) The state of a person who is owned by another person, 74.

sugarcane (ˈshůg-ər-ˌkān) A tall grass whose stalks contain a juice from which sucrose is made, 71.

terrace (ˈter-əs) A raised land area with the top flattened or leveled, 48.

tuber (ˈt(y)ü-bər) The underground storage stem of a plant, 47.

vaccine (vak-ˈsēn) A medicine or preparation that helps keep people from getting an infectious disease, 27.

INDEX

PHOTOGRAPH AND TEXT CREDITS

Chapter 1
photographs: p. 4: Gerry Ellis/The Wildlife Collection; p. 7: courtesy of the Library of Congress; p. 8: Scala/Art Resource, New York; pp. 9 and 10: North Wind Picture Archives.

Chapter 2
photographs: p. 14: Museo Nacional de Antropologia, Mexico; p. 16: New York Public Library; p. 17, margin: Tom Dillehay; p. 18: Tom Falley/Allstock; p. 21: from Guamán Poma de Ayala, *Nueva Cronica*, courtesy of Det Kongelige Bibliotek, Copenhagen; p. 22: Fred Mang, Jr./National Park Service; p. 23, margin: Department of Anthropology, Smithsonian Institution, Catalogue No. 82-15200; p. 23: Montana Historical Society, Helena, Montana; p. 25, top: Bill E. Hess/©National Geographic Society; p. 25, margin: courtesy of the New York State Museum.

Chapter 3
photographs: p. 26: from the *Florentine Codex*, courtesy of the Peabody Museum, Harvard University; p. 29: Culver Pictures; p. 30: reprinted with permission from *Lienzo de Tlaxcala*, ©Ed Castle/courtesy of Smithsonian Institution; p. 31: John Verano/courtesy of Countway Library, Harvard Medical School; p. 32: John Verano; p. 33: Smithsonian Institution, National Museum of the American Indian; p. 34: Smithsonian Institution, Photo No. 3438.

Chapter 4
photographs: p. 36: courtesy of National Corn Growers Association; p. 38, margin: from Guamán Poma de Ayala, *Nueva Cronica*, courtesy of Det Kongelige Bibliotek, Copenhagen; p. 38: David Alan Harvey/©National Geographic Society; p. 40: Jerry McElroy/corn courtesy of Larry Benner, Colorado State University Cooperative Extension; p. 41: Dumbarton Oaks Research Library and Collections, Washington, D.C.; p. 42: North Wind Picture Archives; p. 43: Jerry McElroy; p. 44: Larry Benner/Colorado State University Cooperative Extension; p. 45: courtesy of National Corn Growers Association; p. 45, margin: Jerry McElroy.

Chapter 5
photographs: p. 46: courtesy of The National Potato Board; p. 48: Chip Clark; p. 49, margin: John Verano/pottery courtesy of National Museum of Natural History, Smithsonian Institution; p. 49: Ron Robbins; p. 50: from Guamán Poma de Ayala, *Nueva Cronica*, courtesy of Det Kongelige Bibliotek, Copenhagen; p. 51: Collections: State Museum, Kröller-Müller, Otterlo, The Netherlands; p. 52: Bibliothèque Nationale, Paris; p. 53, margin: Kenneth W. Knutson/Colorado State University Cooperative Extension; p. 54: courtesy of the Library of Congress; p. 57, both: courtesy of The National Potato Board.
text: p.55: letter from Patrick Murphy, New York, to his mother in Ireland, Sept. 15, 1885.

Chapter 6
photographs: p. 58: Thomas A. Wiewandt/DRK Photo; p. 60: North Wind Picture Archives; p. 61: Fernando Suárez Gonzáles/Archivo de Indias; p. 61, margin: Bancroft Library, University of California, Berkeley; p. 62: North Wind Picture Archives; p. 63: from José Cisneros, *Riders Across the Centuries* ©1984 by Texas Western Press, reproduced with permission from the publisher; p. 64: Jeff Taylor/Lewiston (Idaho) *Morning Tribune*; p. 65: Tom McHugh/Photo Researchers; p. 65, margin: Adolf Hungry Wolf; 67: *Gauchos in a Horse Corral* by James Walker, courtesy of the Thomas Gilcrease Institute of American History and Art, Tulsa, Oklahoma; p. 68, both: courtesy of the Library of Congress; p. 69: courtesy of the American Quarter Horse Association.
text: pp. 65-66: Beverly Hungry Wolf, *The Ways of My Grandmothers*, ©1980 Beverly Hungry Wolf (William Morrow, NY, 1982).

Chapter 7

photographs: p. 70: North Wind Picture Archives; p. 72: from John Baptiste Labat, *Nouveau voyage aux isles de l'Amérique,* vol. 3 (Paris, 1722), courtesy of John Carter Brown Library, Brown University; p. 72, margin: courtesy of the New York Historical Society, New York City; p. 73: courtesy of the Library of Congress; p. 75: North Wind Picture Archives; p. 78: "Going to Market, Constant Spring Road," from A. Duperly and Son, *Picturesque Jamaica* (Kingston, 1902), courtesy of Harvard College Library; p. 78, margin: French West Indies Tourist Board; p. 79: Paul O. Boisvert.

text: p. 79: reprinted with permission of Atheneum Publishers, an imprint of Macmillan Publishing Company, from *Iron Pots and Wooden Spoons* by Jessica B. Harris. Copyright ©1989 by Jessica B. Harris.

Chapter 8

photographs: p. 80: NASA; p. 82: Jerry McElroy; p. 83: Carlye Calvin; p. 85: Rich Buzzelli/Stock Imagery; p. 86: Dirk Gillian, 1990/Journalism Services, Inc., all rights reserved; p. 86, margin: Daniel Gotshall/ Visuals Unlimited; p. 87: George Ancona/ International Stock Photography Ltd.; p. 88: AP/Wide World Photos.

text: p. 85: quote by Tom McMillan, Canadian Environmental Minister.